Three Generations of Cajun and Creole Cooking from the Gulf Coast

FAVRE FAMILY COOKBOOK
By The Favre Family

An Addax Book
Taylor Trade Publishing
Lanham • New York • Dallas • Boulder • Toronto • Oxford

An Addax Book

Published by Taylor Trade Publishing
An imprint of The Rowman & Littlefield Publishing Group, Inc.
4501 Forbes Boulevard, Suite 200
Lanham, Maryland 20706

Copyright © 1999 by Favre Management Group
First Taylor Trade Publishing edition 2005

Coordinated by Michelle Zwickle-Washington
Edited by Nelson Elliott
Cover design by Laura Bolter
Design by Randy Breeden
Select photos by Gary Carson

Distributed by National Book Network

Library of Congress Cataloging-in-Publication Data

Favre family cookbook : three generations of Cajun and Creole
cooking from the Gulf Coast / by Favre Management Corporation.
     p. cm.
   ISBN 1-886110-75-1 (hardcover)
     1. Cookery, American—Louisiana style. 2. Cookery, Cajun. 3.
Cookery, Creole. I. Favre Management Corporation.
   TX715.2.L68 F38 1999   99-16957
   641.59763—dc21   CIP

⊖™ The paper used in this publication meets the minimum requirements of
American National Standard for Information Sciences—Permanence of
Paper for Printed Library Materials, ANSI/NISO Z39.48–1992.
Manufactured in the United States of America.

DEDICATION

To all members of the Favre family both here with us today and those that have come before, whose heritage we value and traditions and memories we cherish. To all of our family and new and old friends, with whom we will continue to share our good times and good food.

Our great-grandparents, Ernest Favre and Winona Favre, instilled a love of food in our family three generations ago. Even with the job of rearing four sons and three daughters, they always had a big pot of something on the stove. Sunday was the day for roast and spaghetti and, usually, a banana pudding. The aroma of that food simmering on the stove is still a pleasant, unforgettable memory for those fortunate enough to have enjoyed their culinary creations.

Of the three sons born to Ernest and Winona, one of them was our grandpa (we called him "Pawpaw"), Alvin Ernest Favre, a full-blooded Choctaw Indian, as was the rest of the family. He was a quiet, yet forceful influence in all of our lives. Pawpaw was best known for his talents on the barbecue. Every holiday Pawpaw would start the grill early in the morning. He would then barbecue meat very slowly. His cooking was always a treat - we miss his delectable ribs. But most of all, we miss Pawpaw, who passed away on March 6, 1998, less than two hours after his 80th birthday. We will always remember him taking us grandkids to Ladner's grocery on Sunday to buy us a root beer.

Scott and Jeff Favre

CONTENTS

4

ACKNOWLEDGMENTS

Our thanks go to:

— Rhonda Favre and Morgan Kowalski for their endless hours of work and patience with this book.

— Irvin and Bonita Favre, the best parents a child could ask for, who made all of this possible.

Our family and friends who participated by giving us family recipes, stories, pictures and time.

— Local restaurants and the Brennan family, especially Dick and Dickie Brennan & Co. for their participation and help.

— Addax Publishing for their support and help throughout this project.

— And, finally, The Good Lord, who has given us a wonderful life with great friends and families.

Scott & Jeff Favre

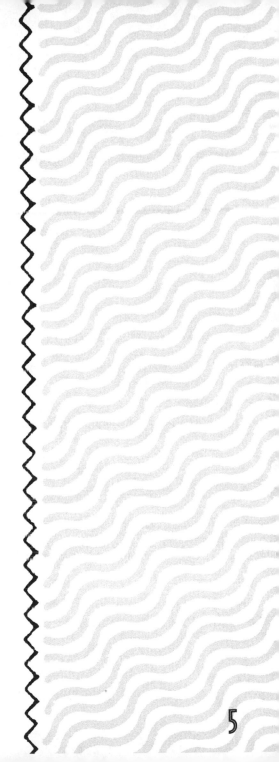

CONTRIBUTORS
(Alphabetical by first name)

ALVIN FAVRE (deceased) was the father of Irvin, Jimbo, Janet, Rock and Kay Kay and the grandfather of Scott, Brett, Jeff, and Brandi Favre; Jan and David Peterson; Neal Favre.

AUDREY LYONS, sister of Alvin Favre; great aunt to Scott, Brett, Jeff and Brandi. She resides in Valparaiso, FL.

BONITA FAVRE is the wife of Irvin Favre, mother of Scott, Brett, Jeff and Brandi and grandmother of Brittany, Dylan and Jade; daughter of Bennie French, Sr. (deceased) and Izella (Meemaw) French. A graduate of St. Joseph Academy, Perkinston Jr. College, and has a B.S. in health, physical education and recreation and an M.S. in special education from the University of Southern Mississippi. Bonita taught PE, general biology and special education, and coached girl's basketball before retiring in 1994. She reigned as queen of St. Paul carnival in 1996, having raised $62,300, along with her king, Leonard Bentz and the members of the Bentz-Favre team, for St. Paul Catholic school. She is a member of the St. Williams Catholic Church.

BRANDI FAVRE is the daughter of Irvin and Bonita and younger sister of Scott, Brett, and Jeff. She is a 1995 graduate of Hancock High School and will graduate in August from the University of South Alabama with a major in broadcast journalism. Brandi was Miss Mississippi American teen in 1992 and was active in basketball, softball, cheerleading and swimming.

BRETT FAVRE, second son of Irvin and Bonita Favre, brother of Scott, Jeff and Brandi, husband of Deanna Favre and father of Brittany Favre. Brett is a 1987 graduate of Hancock North Central High School and attended the University of Southern Mississippi with a major in special education. Brett was a four-year starter for the USM Golden Eagles, where he holds numerous records. He was drafted in the 2nd round of the 1991 NFL draft by the Atlanta Falcons and traded to the Green Bay Packers in 1992. He has been the starting quarterback for the Green Bay Packers since 1992 and is three-time MVP of the National Football League and led the Packers to the Super Bowl title following the 1996 season. He and his family live in Green Bay, WI, and Hattiesburg, MS.

BRITTANY FAVRE is the granddaughter of Irvin and Bonita Favre and daughter of Brett and Deanna Favre. Brittany will be a fifth grader, attending school in Green Bay, WI and Oak Grove, MS. She plays softball and enjoys swimming, boating and skating.

CHAD FAVRE is a high school friend of Jeff Favre. They also played sports together in high school.

CHRISTY PETERSON is the wife of David Peterson, cousin of Scott, Brett, Jeff and Brandi. Before marrying into the Favre family, Christy was readily accused of eating only bird seeds because of her finicky eating habits. However, she is now a full fledged Favre eater, tasting more dishes and having put on a little weight and no longer a scarecrow!

CINDY DOYLE SCHUBERT, mother of Doddle, Bobby and Rhonda. Jeff's mother-in-law.

CLARK HENEGAN is a college friend of Scott and Brett, whom the boys brought home in 1988 for a weekend. He ended up staying for six years and never left. He is now the vice president of administration of the Mississippi Fire Dogs indoor professional football team on the Mississippi Gulf Coast.

DAVID PETERSON, cousin of Scott, Brett, Jeff and Brandi; son of Janet and Kenny Peterson. Dave was probably Brett's first offensive lineman in football, out in the Favre family's homemade football field (an old corn field with lots of grass).

DEANNA FAVRE, wife of Brett Favre and mother of Brittany Favre. Deanna was as tough as the boys when it came to sports. She used to catch Brett's wild curve balls at 80 miles an hour and never fell back. Irvin had to finally make Brett quit showing off to her. She is a 1985 graduate of Hancock North Central, where she played basketball and was the Wendell Ladner Bowl queen. She has a degree in food and nutrition from the University of Southern Mississippi. She came to the Favre family home in 1983 for Scott's 16th birthday party and has been a part of the family ever since. She and Brett were sweethearts for 13 years before marriage.

DEBBIE LAIN was a teaching colleague and friend of Bonita Favre at Hancock North Central High School. Debbie taught home economics and always had something good to taste. Debbie still teachers and resides in Long Beach, MS.

DESTIN BRADY is an old friend of Scott Favre who just got married May 21, 1999, and is frequently made to put on an apron and cook and serve game day specialties. He attended rival Bay High School, but we try to overlook that!

DEWAYNE MALLINI grew up with Bonita Favre in Henderson Point, where the two of them always seemed to get into a few playful fights and trouble. Bonita tells everyone she was going to marry him, but she never could get him tall enough, so she gave him to Irma. His reply is, "If the two of us had gotten married, we wouldn't have had football players, we would have had sumo wrestlers." He and his wife Irma were attendants in Bonita and Irvin's wedding and he is Jeff Favre's Godfather. He is the owner of Mallini's Point Lounge, formerly Bennie French's Tavern, owned by Bonita's parents for over 40 years. They have four children. When they were all little, no one wanted to babysit all four, so Irv and Bonita and Dewayne and Irma spent weekends playing cards, boiling seafood or cooking out with eight youngsters underfoot.

DOROTHY ASMUS along with husband, Arlan, and daughter, Sherry, are Wisconsinites who are now residents of Diamondhead, MS. They have become great family friends. Arlan cooks up a mean fishfry and Dorothy certainly knows how to prepare the appetizers and side dishes.

DYLAN DOYLE, son of Jeff and Rhonda Favre and brother of Jade. He just finished his first year of school. He plays basketball, baseball and loves the WWF, especially Stone Cold. Although not a cook yet, he enjoys making holiday cookies, depending on the Pillsbury dough boy!

FANNIE FAVRE, aunt of Scott, Brett, Jeff and Brandi Favre; wife of Gerald (Jimbo) Favre and mother of Neal Favre. Fannie is an accomplished writer and was editor of the magazine, *Back Porch*.

GENE and LENA MAE BENNETT are Favre family friends. Their daughter, Robin, graduated from high school with Jeff. They are noted for their great Christmas Eve open house with great food and great hospitality. They reside in Kiln, MS.

GLENN ROSE, another Bay High rival and old friend of Scott Favre. Glenn and Scott are known to be seen on the golf course, fishing or cooking up a batch of seafood or something good to eat.

GLORIA JORDAN is a Test Operations Planner for Lockhead Martin at the NASA Space Center in Hancock County and administrative supervisor of Bonita's sister, Layne Bourgeois, at the Space Center.

HELEN and LEONARD BENTZ, Leonard is a childhood friend of Bonita Favre and was her King of St. Paul Carnival in 1996. Helen, Leonard's wife, is a friend and queen of the St. Paul carnival in 1999.

IRMA J. MALLINI is the wife of Dewayne Mallini, friend of Bonita Favre since the 4th grade, and an attendant in the wedding of Irvin and Bonita, and Godmother of Scott Favre. There are not too many people who can boast of having true friends of 45 years, but Irma (better known as "Ricka"), Pat (Ladner) and Bonita have been through so many ups and downs over the years, they can usually tell what is on the others mind and still are bosom buddies through thick and thin!

IRVIN FAVRE is the 2nd son of Alvin Favre, husband of Bonita Favre, father of Scott, Brett, Jeff and Brandi Favre. He is a graduate of Gulfport High School and Perkiston Junior College where he played football and baseball. He has a B.S. degree from the University of Southern Mississippi. He was a pitcher for the USM Golden Eagles in 1966-1967. He began his coaching and teaching career at Long Beach High School, was at St. John High School for two years where his team won the state baseball championship in 1970. From there he went to Hancock North Central High School, where he coached all three sons in football and baseball. In his career he had 120 wins, 88 losses and one tie in football and 129 wins and 91 losses in baseball. He retired from teaching in 1993 and now operates Favre Agricultural Enterprises.

IZELLA FRENCH, mother of Bonita Favre, grandmother of Scott, Brett, Jeff and Brandi. She is better known as Meemaw, not only to her grandchildren, but to most who know her. She and Bonita's dad, Bennie French, Sr., owned and operated Bennie French's Tavern and Bennie French's Restaurant for many years. After the death of her husband she continued to operate the tavern until she sold it to Dewayne Mallini in 1987. In June of 1998, she was honored with a surprise 80th birthday party by her family with over 100 in attendance. She does volunteer work as a pink lady at Garden Park Hospital and is still very active. In fact, she is so active that Bonita has threatened to get a bumper sticker that says, "DO YOU KNOW WHERE YOUR MOTHER IS?"

JAN NATIONS is a cousin of Scott, Brett, Jeff and Brandi Favre; daughter of Kenny and Janet Favre Peterson. Sister of David Peterson. Jan is 15 days older than Scott and they were always getting into things together, like the day they got a tube of Desitin and covered their entire faces. She is the mother of Tristan and Blake and is employed at Triton in Long Beach, MS, where she and husband, Greg, reside.

JEFF FAVRE is the 3rd son of Irvin and Bonita Favre; brother of Scott, Brett and Brandi Favre; husband of Rhonda and father of Dylan Doyle and Jade Favre. He is a 1992 graduate of Hancock High School where he played football and baseball. He has a B.S. degree in accounting from the University of Southern Mississippi and was a defensive back for the USM Golden Eagles. He is employed by the Grand Casino and is co-owner of The Broke Spoke North in Muskego, WI.

JIMBO FAVRE, oldest son of Alvin and Mary Favre; brother of Irvin, Rock and Karen Favre and Janet Peterson; husband of Fannie Favre and father of Neal Favre. He is retired from the Mississippi Power Co. and is notorious for his lemon icebox pies.

JOAN LACOSTE along with her husband, Marvin, is a long-time family friend and resident of Kiln, MS.

JUDY PURSELL is a former college roommate of Bonita Favre. They keep in touch these days by e-mail. She resides in Baton Rouge, LA.

KEN and LESLIE TALLEY are Favre family friends. Bonita met Leslie in 1988 when she was director of the swimming pool in Diamondhead, MS. Leslie has a son named Brett and Bonita heard her call him and told her that she also had a son named Brett and that the little Talley Brett look so much like her son when he was little. They became friends and have remained so. They have four sons, Flynn, Brett, Jordy and Christian and reside in Diamondhead, MS.

KENDALL MICHEL, better known as "Flounder," is an old friend of Scott Favre and also a Bay Rat from rival Bay High. He is known for his fried shrimp.

KRISSY WITTMANN VINCENT is the granddaughter of Bonita Favre's brother, Bennie French, Jr.

LAYNE BOURGEOIS, sister of Bonita Favre and Godmother of Brandi Favre. She is the mother of Daniette and Jace and is employed at Lockhead Martin at NASA Space Center in Hancock County. She resides in Bay St. Louis, MS.

LESLIE LADNER is a Favre family friend and former working colleague of Morgan. Her dad, Jeep, has been the family's plumber and friend for many years.

LINDA FRENCH WITTMANN, daughter of Bonita Favre's brother, Bennie French, Jr. She and her husband Kenny are the parents of Casey, Kim, Chrissy, Kerry and Kyle. She is employed at Memorial Hospital in Gulfport, MS, and resides in Pass Christian, MS.

LLOYD NICAUD, friend of Scott and Brett Favre, graduate of rival St. Stanilaus, most apt to be found on the golf course or fishing, better known to Big Irv as "White Hands." He is married to Kristy, daughter of Lil Ray's proprietors, Ray and Jackie Kidd, and the father of Noah and Grace.

LOUISE FRENCH GREEN, known as "Weezie," is the sister of Bonita Favre. She is married to Jimmy and the mother of Sandy and Sally. Great with desserts!

MALLINI'S POINT LOUNGE, formerly Bennie French's Tavern owned by Bennie and Izella French, mother of Bonita Favre, sold to Dewayne and Irma Mallini, childhood friends of Bonita Favre.

MARK GAMBINO, St. Stanilaus grad and friend of Scott Favre. Gambino has the art of boiling seafood to perfection. Resides in Bay St. Louis, MS.

MARY FAVRE (deceased) was the mother of Irvin, Jimbo, Janet, Rock and Kay Kay and the grandmother of Scott, Brett, Jeff and Brandi Favre, Jan and David Peterson and Neal Favre.

MARY HESS WITTMANN is the wife of Kerry Wittmann, Scott, Brett, Jeff and Brandi's cousin.

MERLE NORFOLK, friend and teaching colleague of Bonita Favre since 1978. Taught Scott Favre in the 7th grade. She and her husband Chuck moved back to Diamondhead, MS, after spending ten years in St. Croix, Virgin Islands. She is very active in numerous organizations in the community and always willing to lend a helping hand. Although not an accomplished cook, she is begging to try her hands in the kitchen. Perhaps the cookbook will help! She has one son, Jeff, and readily answers to "Squirrel" or "Merle the Pearl."

MILTON FAVRE, brother of Alvin Favre.

MITZI FAVRE PALAZZO, daughter of Milton and Peggy Favre and wife of Frank Palazzo. Cousin of Scott, Brett, Jeff and Brandi Favre. Mitzi teaches at a private school in Picayune, MS, and resides in Gulfport, MS.

MONICA LADNER WITTMANN, wife of Casey Wittmann, son of Linda French Wittmann, cousin of Scott, Brett Jeff and Brandi Favre. She is employed at Hancock Bank in Diamondhead, MS, and resides in Pass Christian, MS.

MORGAN KOWALSKI is the fiancee of Scott Favre. She is employed in accounting at Memorial Hospital in Gulfport, MS, and is busy planning a March wedding.

MYRA MARSH, family friend who is always ready to help with any event. She has been designated as candy maker for showers, weddings, etc. Whenever you say go, she is the first to be ready. Married to Gene and mother of one son, Dennis.

MYRA PETERSON is supervisor of the cafeteria at Hancock High School and has fed the Favre family for many years and is a good friend.

NORA SPIKES was the mother of Mary Favre and the grandmother of Scott, Brett, Jeff and Brandi. She was known to then as "NoNo" and could always be depended on to have something good to eat.

PAT LADNER has been a friend of Bonita Favre since the 4th grade. They grew up on Henderson Point where they managed to get into all kinds of endeavors together. She, Irma Mallini and Bonita are the three musketeers! She and Bonita are also very psychic. They will think of each other or happenings simultaneously. She is Brett Favre's Godmother and the author of *Fundamentals of Nursing*. She resides in Metairie, LA, with her husband, Wayne, and is the mother of Kelly, Wayne, Jr., Gretchen and Michael and grandmother of Leah.

PEGGY FAVRE is the wife of Milton Favre, mother of Mitzi Favre Palazzo. She is always coming up with great dishes and desserts for family gatherings.

PEGGY LADNER, Favre family friend, married to Coach Larry Ladner and mother of Scott and Brett's friend, Jay. They are both retired from the University of Southern Mississippi.

PENNY TRIPP is the mother of Christy Peterson, wife of David Peterson, son of Kenny and Janet Favre Peterson.

POPPA SYLVESTER PAGANO resided across the street from Bennie French Family, long-time friend of the family.

RHONDA FAVRE, wife of Jeff and mother of Dylan and Jade. She is a graduate of Hancock High School and played football (yes, football!) against Jeff in junior high school!

ROXANNA HUERTA, friend of Rhonda and Jeff Favre. She is a resident of Milwaukee, WI.

SANDRA SMITH, mother of Scott Favre's fiancé, Morgan Kowalski, and long-time friend of Bonita Favre.

SANDY ADAMS, teaching colleague and good friend of Bonita Favre.

SCOTT FAVRE, 1st son of Irvin and Bonita Favre; brother of Brett, Jeff and Brandi Favre. He is a graduate of Hancock North Central High School where he played football, baseball, basketball and golf. He played football and baseball at Pearl River Junior College and has a degree in special education from the University of Southern Mississippi. He taught school in Atlanta and is now employed as a realtor with Coldwell Banker in Diamondhead, MS. He is engaged to Morgan Kowalski, planning a March, 2000, wedding.

STEVIE HAAS, friend and business partner of Jeff Favre; owner of The Broke Spoke, Kiln, MS.

WILDA MCNATT, friend and teaching colleague of Bonita Favre since 1978. Taught Scott, Brett, Jeff and Brandi Favre. She resides in Picayune, MS.

DANNY AND CANDI WASILENKO friends of Morgan Kowalski, fiancee of Scott Favre.

NADINE PATTON, friend and teaching colleague of Bonita Favre since 1979. Taught Jeff, Rhonda and Brandi Favre.

SCOTT HAAS is a business partner of Jeff Favre. He resides in Kiln, MS.

11

FOREWORD

Recipes are an expression of the individual. They are a reflection of heritage. Food provides a medium for communication with others. It allows us the chance to explore cultures that we might otherwise not have the opportunity to experience. Food nurtures the body, quiets the mind and strengthens the spirit. It is often a centerpiece for some of the most exciting moments. It shares our emotions. Such was the creation of this cookbook. On Christmas day, 1997, when our families came together for a short visit, Scott was challenged by the collective gathering to write a cookbook. The dare was issued to share his cooking skills and ensure we all had the best of his recipes. (Now you have them too!) Whether Scott prepares red beans and rice or Huitres Bienville (Oyster Bienville), the recipe is easy, it takes little time to prepare, and makes you feel like you are dining at the Ritz.

Bonita Favre has been my friend for forty-four years. What memories we have shared through both good and hard times. Showers, birthdays, graduations and weddings are special times to enjoy with family and friends. But when we look back, the best times were just being together as our children grew up. We seized every moment to combine our families and friends. Friday nights were special for high school football games or a friendly bouree (a card) game. With four children each, we always planned the menu well in advance. We would fry catfish, then prepare whatever items our budgets permitted. Appetizers, like shrimp dip and avocado dip, were a must to ensure an uninterrupted card game. The shrimp dip recipe has survived over the years with only one change. We can now make the dip with fresh shrimp, no longer having to open the "little can." The first time I made the dip with real shrimp, Bonita asked for the recipe, even though it was Bonita who had given me the original recipe.

Since the Favres lived in the country, it was our meeting place. The children could play ball, swim, fish and hunt while never leaving the Favre land. Although the children were safe, their personal belongings often had a different fate! Wayne, my oldest son, had spent the weekend, a common happening. When I went to pick him up I inquired about his bag that contained his new tennis shoes and other clothes. As the story went, Irvin "Poppy" Favre had directed the collection of garbage for the dump - all the garbage bags were taken there. However, instead of delivering the garbage to the dump, the bags were somehow tossed into a creek. Off we went to retrieve my child's shoes. At this point the clothes were not considered retrievable. With a ten-foot fishing pole dangling from a bridge, seven adults and ten children tried to fish the bag from the creek. The laughter on the bridge that day is still heard as newcomers are warned not to leave their personal belongings in a bag on the Favre's floor.

Now when we gather to share a good time, Scott, Jeff, Brett (when he is home) and their friends do the majority of the cooking, frying the fish or a well-seasoned turkey, boiling the catch of the day, crabs or crawfish. Bonita and I are still responsible for most of the appetizers, side dishes, and the quality of day, making sure that everyone has a good time.

This book presents a collection of New Orleans' best recipes and the Mississippi Gulf Coast's finest cooking, as prepared and eaten by the Favres and their friends. This cuisine should be eaten and shared with family and friends in an atmosphere of fun, joy and laughter. I sincerely hope that the exceptional quality of this cuisine will tempt all cooks to want to share their recipes and creations with others.

Patricia Ladner
Metairie, LA

3 musketeers, friends for 45 years - Pat Ladner, Irma Mallini and Bonita Favre.

INTRODUCTION

We love to eat. There is nothing better than good cooking, whether its Cajun, Creole or good-old southern cooking. Here on the Mississippi Gulf Coast we have access to the greatest food sources in the world. We have the freshest seafood, including fish, shrimp, crawfish and crabs. (I realize that seafood is served in other areas besides the Gulf Coast, but I truly believe it is our blend of seasonings and preparation that sets us apart.)

My entire family loves to cook. Each person prepares their own dishes for special occasions and on a regular basis. You hear comments such as, "This is good, but not like grandma's," or in my case, Meemaw's! Well, in this cookbook, you will get not only grandma's cooking secrets but also those of other family and friends.

Cajun cooking is exemplified by dark roux and spicy food. Creole cooking is more refined, placing more emphasis on butter and cream.

When I think of Cajun cooking, I want you to think of boiling crawfish or shrimp on the bayou, with alligators in sight and people having a good time. That is the journey we want you to take in the pages to follow. This cookbook also includes favorite recipes and pictures from chefs of restaurants from the Mississippi Gulf Coast. Best of the Coast will be a recommendation of the best places to eat while visiting our beautiful Gulf Coast. Our final chapter will be the Best of the Rest. This chapter is contributed by Dickie Brennan's restaurants. It comes with our recommendation for you to visit their eating establishments nestled in the heart of New Orleans.

Our book is more conversational than grammatical. It is more fun than formal. It comes from our hearts. Let your taste buds be the judge.

Scott Favre
Diamondhead, MS

APPETIZERS

An appetizer is supposed to be a warm-up before the meal. However, there are many occasions where appetizers are in fact, the feasts. Here on the Mississippi Gulf Coast, there is always an event about to take place. Birthdays, showers, weddings, anniversaries, engagements, christenings, Mardi Gras, holidays, festivals, football games - all celebrations. We are always looking for a reason to throw a party. Sometimes just sitting around after someone drops in is a great reason. Before you know it, you are in the kitchen, at the grill or firing up the pot for boiled seafood.

We have a lot of gatherings, which include "bring a dish." Bringing a dish to share is a great way of sampling and acquiring other recipes. Appetizers can be as simple as chips and dip, cheese and crackers, or as elegant as crab stuffed mushrooms or shrimp mold. Let your imagination be your guide, as we have, as many great dishes await you.

Bonita Favre

Artwork of the Mississippi Gulf Coast by John & Tricia McDonald is featured as opening art for a number of the chapters.

John, a native of the Mississippi coast, grew up in the quaint little town of Pass Christian. He and his wife, Tricia, specialize in scenes which depict the beauty and history of the coastal communities from Bay Saint Louis to Ocean Springs.

Full color prints of the artwork preceding each chapter may be purchased by contacting Coastal Impressions, P.O. Box 541, Pass Christian, MS, 39571, or by phone at 228-452-3049.

Thank you from the Favre family.

Sea Angel
Bayou Portage (Po-tash) feeds into the Bay of Saint Louis, Mississippi. Jimmy Bradley, his wife Diane, and their trawler the Sea Angel, all live in a wonderfully secluded spot on the bayou just north of Pass Christian.

Rotten Bayou during Hurricane Georges.

Rotten Bayou is actually "Beneshewah." It became known as Rotten Bayou when the Indians would clean their game and throw the pelts in the water.

MAMA BO'S SHRIMP DIP

8   ounces Philadelphia cream cheese, softened
½   small onion, chopped
    Dash of Worcestershire sauce
    Dash of Tabasco sauce to taste
2   tablespoons mayonnaise
2   teaspoons dried parsley flakes
1   4-ounce can shrimp, or freshly boiled shrimp
Evaporated milk, enough to dilute to desired consistency

Blend cream cheese and onion in food processor. Add Worcestershire sauce, Tabasco sauce, mayonnaise and parsley. Blend. Add shrimp and juice. Do not blend very long. You may want to use pulse control. Add evaporated milk to thin to desired consistency. Serve with Fritos.

Serves 4 to 6

Bonita Favre

STUFFED MUSHROOMS WITH CRABMEAT

8   large mushrooms
1   cup lump crabmeat, cooked or uncooked
2   tablespoons bread crumbs
2   tablespoons onions, finely chopped
1   teaspoon salt
1   teaspoon pepper
2   tablespoons parsley
1   egg, beaten
¼   cup bread crumbs
¼   cup Parmesan cheese

Rinse mushrooms and remove stems. In a bowl, mix crabmeat, bread crumbs, onions, salt, pepper and parsley. Add egg and mix well. Fill mushroom caps with mixture and sprinkle with bread crumbs and cheese. Bake in oven at 350° F for 20 minutes.

Serves 4 to 6

Scott Favre

CATFISH BEIGNETS

2 tablespoons vegetable oil
½ cup onions, chopped
1 tcaspoon salt
½ teaspoon cayenne pepper
1 pound catfish, cut in ½ inch pieces
1 teaspoon garlic, chopped
¼ cup green onions, chopped
3 eggs, beaten
1 ½ cups milk
2 teaspoons baking powder
3 ¼ cups all-purpose flour
  Vegetable shortening for frying
  Remoulade sauce (refer to page 170)

Heat oil in large skillet. Add onions and sauté for 3 minutes. Season with salt and cayenne. Add catfish and sauté for 2-3 minutes. Stir in garlic and green onions. Sauté for 1 minute. Remove from heat and cool.

Mix eggs, milk and baking powder. Add flour, ¼ cup at a time, beating well until the batter is smooth. Fold in catfish mixture.

Heat shortening in a deep fryer or a large, heavy saucepan to 350° F. Drop heaping spoonfuls of batter into hot oil, one at a time. When beignets pop to the surface, roll them around with a slotted spoon to brown evenly. Drain grease and serve with remoulade dipping sauce.

Serves 4 to 6

Scott Favre

STRAWBERRY CHEESE BALL

2	cups Cheddar cheese, grated
1	cup pecans, chopped
1	cup mayonnaise
1	small onion, grated
	Dash cayenne pepper
	Dash black pepper
1	jar strawberry preserves

Mix all ingredients except preserves. Mold into a ring and chill in refrigerator. When ready to serve, fill center with strawberry preserves. Serve with crackers.

Serves 6 to 8

Nadine Patton

Brett Favre loved football even at a very young age.

HOT BROCCOLI DIP

3	stalks broccoli, finely chopped
½	cup celery, finely chopped
½	large onion, finely chopped
1	8-ounce can mushrooms pieces
2	tablespoons butter
1	10-ounce package frozen chopped broccoli
1	can cream of mushroom soup
1	roll garlic cheese
	Tortilla chips

Sauté fresh broccoli, celery, onion and mushroom pieces in butter. Cook frozen broccoli as directed and drain well. Add mushroom soup to above ingredients. Melt cheese in double broiler. Combine all ingredients in chafing dish to serve. Dip with corn or tortilla chips.

Serves 4 to 6

Morgan Kowalski

PICKLED OKRA

2   pounds tender fresh okra
5   pods hot red or green peppers
5   cloves garlic, peeled
1   quart white vinegar
½   cup water
6   tablespoons salt
1   tablespoon celery or mustard seed

Wash okra. Pack okra in 5 hot sterilized pint jars. Put 1 pepper and 1 garlic clove in each. Boil remaining ingredients, pour over okra and seal. Let stand 8 weeks at room temperature before using.

Serves 4 to 6

Bonita Favre

ARTICHOKE DIP

2   large cans artichoke hearts, quartered
1   cup mayonnaise
1   tablespoon garlic powder
1   teaspoon paprika
1   cup Parmesan cheese
3   dashes hot sauce

Mix all ingredients together in a 1-quart casserole dish. Bake 20 to 25 minutes at 350° F until brown. Serve with crackers.

Serves 4 to 6

Bonita Favre

OYSTER DIP

1	small onion, finely chopped
½	green bell pepper, finely chopped
½	cup green onions, chopped
1	clove garlic, minced
1	8 ½-ounce can mushrooms
½	stick butter
2	tablespoons flour
1	pint half and half
1	pint oysters

Sauté onion, bell pepper, green onions, garlic and mushrooms in butter until tender. Add flour, half and half and oysters. Cook over medium heat until thickened. Serve warm with crackers or chips.

Serves 4 to 6

Jeff Favre

STUFFED PISTOLETTES

2	tablespoons butter
4	cloves garlic, minced
1	small onion, chopped
1	small green bell pepper, chopped
2	tablespoons flour
1	teaspoon salt
1	teaspoon black pepper
1	pound pre-cooked crawfish tails
1	teaspoon Worcestershire sauce
1	cup Parmesan cheese, grated
2	cups evaporated milk
8	pistolettes

Melt butter over low heat. Add garlic, onion and bell pepper, sauté until soft. Add flour, salt and pepper. Add crawfish and cook for 10 minutes. Then mix in remaining ingredients except pistolettes, remove from heat, and let thicken. Spoon out pistolette and stuff with mixture. Bake at 325° F for 10 minutes or deep fry in oil for 3-5 minutes.

Serves 6 to 8

Scott Favre

HOT CRAB DIP

2   cans mushroom soup
1   pound lump crabmeat
1   teaspoon Worcestershire sauce
1   teaspoon lemon juice
½   cup Parmesan cheese
½   cup green onions, chopped
    Dash of salt
    Dash of pepper

Heat soup and add remaining ingredients. Keep warm.
Serve with crackers or chips.

Serves 4 to 6

Scott Favre

CRAWFISH DIP

1   stick butter or margarine
½   cup green bell pepper, chopped
1   cup onion, chopped
1   can Rotel tomatoes, diced
1   can cream of mushroom soup
1   16-ounce box of Velveeta cheese
1   pound pre-cooked crawfish tails
3   tablespoons green onions, chopped
    Salt to taste
    Cayenne pepper to taste

Heat butter over medium heat in large skillet. Sauté bell pepper and
onion until wilted. Add Rotel tomatoes, stirring occasionally, add
soup and let cook. Add cheese and let melt completely, add crawfish
and let cook until crawfish are heated through. Add green onions,
salt and pepper, and serve with any kind of chips or crackers.

Serves 6 to 8

Monica Ladner Wittmann

**Irvin Favre was a
pitcher for the University of
Southern Mississippi.**

21

PEPPER JELLY

Important! Wear rubber gloves while handling peppers.

¼	cup jalapeno peppers, IMPORTANT! - seeded and finely chopped
1 ⅓	cups green bell pepper, chopped
6 ½	cups sugar
1 ½	cups wine cider vinegar
1	small bottle of Certo
2 or 3	tablespoons green or red food coloring

Mix green and jalapeno peppers with sugar and vinegar. Bring to boil. Boil for 1 minute then turn down heat. Cook about 5 minutes, then add food coloring and Certo. Put into sterilized jelly glasses. Seal. Serve pepper jelly over cream cheese with crackers.

Serves 6 to 8

Bonita Favre

ARTICHOKE BALLS

3	cloves garlic, pureed
3	tablespoons olive oil
2	8 ½-ounce cans artichoke hearts, drained and mashed (you may use a food processor)
2	eggs, slightly beaten
1	cup Parmesan cheese, grated
1	cup Italian bread crumbs

Sauté garlic in olive oil. Add artichoke hearts and eggs, cook over low heat about five minutes, stirring constantly. Remove from heat and add ½ cup cheese and ½ cup bread crumbs. Roll into bite size balls, using about 1 teaspoon of mixture. Then roll in equal amounts of breadcrumbs and cheese. Chill 1 hour, or until firm.

Serves 6 to 8

Bonita Favre

SHRIMP COCKTAIL

2	tablespoons liquid crab boil
½	gallon water
2	tablespoons salt
1	tablespoon cayenne pepper
1	tablespoon lemon juice
½	pound (26-30 count per pound) shrimp, tails remaining
	Lettuce
	Tomato wedges
	Sprig parsley

In a small pot add liquid crab boil, water, salt, cayenne pepper and lemon juice. Bring to a boil, add shrimp and boil for two minutes. Remove pot from fire and let the shrimp soak for 15 minutes. Peel shrimp and leave the tails on.

Place shrimp on a bed of lettuce on cocktail dish, add tomato wedges and sprig parsley. Serve with cocktail sauce (refer to page 45) and crackers.

Serves 6 to 8

Rhonda Favre

23

MUSHROOM CREAM-FILLED PATTY SHELLS

¾   cup butter or margarine
4   large onions, finely chopped
2   tablespoons parsley, minced, preferably flat leaf
2   tablespoons chives, chopped
½   pound fresh mushrooms, finely chopped
3   tablespoons all-purpose flour
¾   cup whipping cream
¼   teaspoon dried thyme
¼   teaspoon cayenne pepper
1 ½   teaspoons black pepper
1   teaspoon salt
1   tablespoon fresh lemon juice
24   baked patty shells
2   tablespoons Parmesan cheese, grated

Melt ¼ cup butter in a heavy 10-inch skillet, over medium heat. Add onions, parsley and chives. Cook until wilted, about 3 minutes. Stir in mushrooms. Cook 10 minutes or until liquid evaporates. Sprinkle flour over mixture and stir until blended. Cook 2 minutes stirring; mixture will be dry. Stir in cream, thyme, cayenne, black pepper, salt and lemon juice, stirring 5 minutes or until thickened. Reduce heat to low. Preheat oven to 350° F. Place shells on ungreased baking sheet. Fill each with filling. Top with cheese and a teaspoon of butter. Bake in preheated oven until filling is bubbly. Serve hot.

Serves 12 to 14

Bonita Favre

Mawmaw with
USM Golden Eagle.

CANDIED BACON

1   pound bacon, cut into 3 inch strips
   Light brown sugar

Line a jelly roll pan with foil. Sprinkle brown sugar (enough to cover bottom). Lay bacon on top. Bake at 300° F until bacon is brown on one side, turn over and brown the other side. About ½ hour on each side. Periodically drain bacon of grease. Cool bacon on brown paper bag.

Serves 4 to 6

Dorothy Asmus

SHRIMP MOLD

1	8-ounce can tomato soup
1	8-ounce package cream cheese
1 ½	cups water
2	envelopes of Knox gelatin
1 ½	cups (fresh or canned) shrimp (or crab)
1	cup mayonnaise
½	cup celery, chopped
½	cup green pepper, chopped
¼	cup green onions, chopped
1	tablespoon Worcestershire sauce
½	teaspoon salt
1	teaspoon mayonnaise

Bring soup to boil then add cream cheese and dissolve. In another pan, boil water and mix in gelatin. Add to soup. Mix in the remaining ingredients, except the 1 teaspoon of mayonnaise. Grease mold with the 1 teaspoon of mayonnaise. Pour mixture into mold. Chill until set.

Serves 6 to 8

Bonita Favre

AVOCADO DIP

1	small onion, diced
1	average size tomato, diced
¼	a bunch of cilantro, diced
5	avocados, diced
	Canned jalapenos and vinegar, to taste
½	lime
	Salt to taste

Mix onion, tomato, cilantro and avocado. Add jalapenos and vinegar in can. Squeeze ½ lime and add salt to taste.

Serves 6 to 8

Roxanna Huerta

GREEN SALSA

½   cup water
4   fresh jalapenos, diced
5   tomatillos (green tomatoes), diced
½   small onion, diced
¼   a bunch of cilantro, diced
1   clove of garlic, minced
1   chile de arbal
1   teaspoon salt

Boil jalapenos and tomatillas in ½ cup water until jalapenos start turning yellow. Blend jalapenos, tomatillas, onions, cilantro, garlic, chile de arbal, salt and water from jalapenos and tomatillas in a blender. Use intermittent chop mode until chunky.

Serves 6 to 8

Roxanna Huerta

RED SALSA

½   cup water
5   fresh jalapenos
2   average size tomatoes, diced
1   clove garlic, minced
1   teaspoon salt

Boil jalapenos and tomatoes in ½ cup water until jalapenos start turning yellow. Put jalapenos, tomatoes, garlic, salt and water from jalapenos and tomatoes in blender. Use intermittent chop mode until salsa is chunky.

Serves 6 to 8

Roxanna Huerta

FRUIT DIP

1 ½ tablespoons cornstarch
½   cup sugar
1   cup crushed pineapple
1   tablespoon lemon juice
¾   cup water
1   small container whipped cream

Combine cornstarch and sugar. Stir in crushed
pineapple, lemon juice and water. Bring to a boil,
stirring constantly. Boil until clear. (It will be a yellow
color.) Cool completely and combine with whipped
cream. Serve with fresh fruit.

Serves 6 to 8

Myra Peterson

MOM'S HAM ROLLS

8   ounces Philadelphia cream cheese, room temperature
1   tablespoon mayonnaise
1   green onion (green part only) snipped with kitchen
    shears
1   teaspoon Tony Chachere's seasoning
    Dash of parsley
8   slices honey ham
2   tablespoons onion, finely chopped (optional)
    Black or green olives to taste (optional)
    Pecans to taste (optional)

Cream mayonnaise with cream cheese. Add other ingredients, except
the ham, and mix well. Spread the mixture on ham slices and roll up.
Refrigerate until firm. Slice with a sharp knife into rolls before serving. I sometimes add chopped olives (black or green), chopped
pecans or any other variation that tempts your taste buds.

Serves 12 to 14

Bonita Favre

Jeff holding the line at age 4.

MARINATED CRAB CLAWS

16 ounces crab claw fingers, cooked
8   ounces Italian dressing
1   onion, sliced
½   green bell pepper, cut into strips
1   clove garlic, minced
½   teaspoon sugar
1   teaspoon Worcestershire sauce

Mix all ingredients except the crab claws. Put crab in bowl and pour marinade over the crab. Seal with lid and refrigerate overnight. Turn the bowl over periodically, so that the marinade covers the crabs. When ready to serve, remove crab fingers and place in a shallow serving bowl, in circular fashion, standing with shell up. You can put some of the marinade in a bowl to keep the crabs from drying out, if they last that long!!! The longer they marinate, the better they are.

Serves 6 to 8

Bonita Favre

SPINACH DIP

1   10-ounce package chopped spinach, cooked and drained well
1   package Knorr's vegetable soup mix
8   ounces sour cream
1   cup mayonnaise
1   can water chestnuts, chopped
3   green onions, chopped
1   round Hawaiian bread loaf

Mix all ingredients except bread and chill. Scoop the bread out and put spinach dip in the center. Serve with Wheat Thins.

Serves 6 to 8

Brandi Favre

HANKY PANKIES

1   pound ground beef
1   pound sausage
1   pound Velveeta cheese, diced
1   tablespoon Italian seasoning
½   teaspoon garlic salt
½   teaspoon Worcestershire sauce
1   loaf sliced party rye bread

Brown ground beef and sausage in skillet and drain. Add remaining ingredients, except bread, stirring until cheese is melted. Spread on bread. Bake at 400° F for 12 minutes or until bubbly or broil for 5 minutes. Yields about 10 appetizers.

Note: These can be frozen on cookie sheets before baking, then placed in plastic bags and returned to freezer. It is not necessary to thaw before baking.

Serves 4 to 6

Sandy Adams

JALAPENO CHEESE DIP

4   tablespoons flour
½   stick butter
1   heaping teaspoon paprika
1   heaping teaspoon chili powder
¼   teaspoon dry mustard
1   tablespoon catsup
¾   teaspoon ground cumin
1   teaspoon jalapeno liquid
¾   teaspoon garlic salt
2   pods jalapeno peppers, diced
1-1½ cups milk
¾   pound Velveeta cheese, diced

Cook flour and butter in saucepan until butter is melted. Add remaining ingredients, reserving ½ cup milk until needed, if dip is too thick. Cook until cheese is melted. Serve with Fritos or Doritos.

Serves 4 to 6

Brett Favre

29

SALADS & DRESSINGS

Summertime on the Mississippi Gulf Coast has always been a great time to enjoy a meal of a cool, crisp salad, with crackers and a tall glass of iced tea. I used to say that a salad was just green lettuce topped with garden ripe vegetables and your favorite dressing. But with the emergence of the casino industry and their endless buffets, salads have become major meals. The only necessary additional ingredients are fresh Gulf seafood and imagination. Remember, there are no limits. Fresh greens, vegetables, pasta, seafood, eggs, relishes, pickles, peppers, fruits and meats can be used to compliment each other and create very delectable dishes!

Bonita Favre

Shoofly
Bay Saint Louis, Mississippi

These beautifully designed structures were a common sight along the Gulf Coast during the early part of the century.

Not only did they add beauty to the local landscape, they served a very important purpose during the insect season.

At some point in time, someone discovered that mosquitoes and some flies were found to inhabit the landscape just a few feet above the ground.

The Shoofly was built just high enough to avoid many of these unwanted visitors.

AUNT IRMA'S SPINACH SALAD

1   pound fresh spinach leaves, washed and torn into bite size pieces
1   purple or vidalia onion, diced
1   10-ounce pack fresh mushrooms, sliced
3   hard boiled eggs, chopped
8   strips bacon fried crisp, crumbled
8   ounces Italian dressing
     Fresh grated Parmesan cheese to taste
     Croutons to taste

½ hour before serving, marinate mushrooms and onions in Italian dressing. When ready to serve, toss spinach with eggs, bacon, marinade, croutons and cheese. Serve.

Serves 6 to 8

Irma J. Mallini

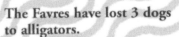

The Favres have lost 3 dogs to alligators.

MAWMAW'S AMBROSIA SALAD

1   cup oranges, peeled and diced
2   bananas, peeled and sliced
½   cup seedless grapes
⅓   cup pitted dates, cut up
3   tablespoons lemon juice
¾   cup whipped cream
1   cup mayonnaise
¼   cup flaked coconut

Combine fruits. Sprinkle with lemon juice and chill. Fold whipped cream into mayonnaise. Fold into fruit mixture. Top with coconut.

Serves 6 to 8

Mary (Mawmaw) Favre

31

BEAN SALAD

1	16-ounce can cut green beans
1	16-ounce can cut wax beans
1	15-ounce can red kidney beans
½	cup green bell peppers, chopped
½	cup onions, chopped
½	cup sugar
⅔	cup vinegar
⅓	cup olive oil
1	teaspoon salt
¼	teaspoon pepper

Drain beans and combine. Add green peppers and onions. Mix sugar, vinegar and oil together. Pour over vegetables. Add salt and pepper, toss. Refrigerate overnight. Toss well before serving.

Serves 6 to 8

Jan Nations

MOM'S TACO SALAD

1	pound lean ground beef
1	15-ounce can kidney beans, drained
¼	teaspoon salt
	Pepper to taste
1	8-ounce jar mild taco sauce
1	onion, chopped
3	tomatoes, chopped
1	head lettuce, chopped
1	avocado, diced (optional)
4	ounces Cheddar cheese, shredded
1	14 ½-ounce bag of Taco Doritos
8	ounces thousand island dressing

Brown ground beef, add beans, salt and pepper. Add taco sauce, then drain and cool. Toss onion, tomatoes, lettuce and avocado with grated cheese. Crush 1 bag of Doritos and add to lettuce mixture. Mix with beef. Add thousand island dressing just before serving.

Serves 6 to 8

Bonita Favre

WATERGATE SALAD

We couldn't do a cookbook without including this recipe, as it was a favorite of our late paternal grandmother, Mary Favre, Mawmaw!

1   large container of Cool Whip
1   package pistachio instant pudding mix
1   8 ½-ounce can pineapple tidbits
2   cups miniature marshmallows
1   cup pecans, chopped (optional)

Put all ingredients into a large bowl. Mix well. Chill for 4 hours.

Serves 6 to 8

Mary Favre

AUNT PEGGY'S LAYERED LETTUCE SALAD

1   medium head of lettuce, chopped or torn into pieces
1   head cauliflower, chopped or torn into small pieces
½   cup red onion, thinly sliced
1   cup broccoli, chopped into small pieces
1   10-ounce package frozen green peas
1   bunch fresh spinach leaves
1   package ranch salad dressing mix, follow directions on package
⅓   cup shredded Cheddar cheese
½   cup bacon bits

In a large container, layer the first six ingredients. Pour the mixed salad dressing over the vegetables. Sprinkle with cheese and bacon bits. Refrigerate overnight.

Serves 6 to 8

Peggy Favre

AUNT PEGGY'S CORN SALAD

2	cans shoepeg corn
1	large onion, chopped
1	large green bell pepper, chopped
2	large tomatoes, chopped
3	tablespoons mayonnaise
	Salt to taste
	Pepper to taste

Mix all ingredients and refrigerate for 4 hours.

Serves 4 to 6

Peggy Favre

LAYERED GARDEN PASTA SALAD

1	package (7 or 8 ounces) macaroni shells
½	cup green onions, sliced (with tops)
¼	cup Bac O's
1	cup mayonnaise
¼	cup real lemon juice
3	tablespoons Parmesan cheese
1	teaspoon sugar
½	teaspoon garlic powder
4	cups salad greens
1	medium zucchini, washed and sliced
1	cup cauliflower, sliced
1	cup broccoli florets
2	medium tomatoes cut into wedges

Cook macaroni as directed. Drain. Rinse with cold water and drain again. Stir together macaroni, onions and 2 tablespoons Bac O's in medium bowl. Mix mayonnaise, lemon juice, cheese, sugar and garlic powder. In a 3 ½ quart salad bowl, layer salad greens, macaroni mixture, zucchini, cauliflower, broccoli and tomatoes. Pour dressing evenly over top. Cover and refrigerate at least 2 hours. Sprinkle with the 2 tablespoons Bac O's just before serving.

Serves 6 to 8

Mitzi Favre Palazzo

UNCLE JIMBO'S POTATO SALAD

3   pounds boiled potatoes, cubed or mashed
3   boiled eggs, chopped
¼   cup sweet pickle relish
¼   cup green olives, chopped
½   cup onions, chopped
3   tablespoons Creole mustard with horseradish
½   cup mayonnaise, or enough to make the potato salad creamy

Mix all ingredients. Serve with red beans and rice (refer to page 135) or make a potato salad sandwich. A dash of Tabasco sauce makes it even better.

Serves 8 to 10

Jimbo Favre

KAY KAY'S KICKING KOLE SLAW

1   medium head cabbage, shredded
4   carrots, peeled and grated
2   medium green bell peppers, thinly sliced
1   medium onion, thinly sliced
1   teaspoon garlic, minced
1   cup sour cream
2   tablespoons sugar
1 ½   teaspoons vinegar
1 ½   tablespoons mayonnaise
½   teaspoon salt
¼   teaspoon pepper

In large mixing bowl, toss cabbage, carrots, peppers and onion. In another bowl, blend together remaining ingredients, pour over cabbage and toss well.

Serves 6 to 8

Karen Favre

Brittany Favre and Karen "Kay Kay" Favre

35

AUNT LAYNE'S RANCH DRESSING

½ teaspoon onion, finely chopped
¼ teaspoon garlic powder
½ teaspoon dried parsley
1 teaspoon dried or fresh chives
  Salt to taste
1 cup buttermilk
1 cup mayonnaise

Mix the seasonings with the buttermilk in a small bowl. Blend in the mayonnaise until smooth. Refrigerate for 4 hours.

Serves 6 to 8

Layne Bourgeois

Sisters Bonita and Layne

MOM'S THOUSAND ISLAND DRESSING

1 cup mayonnaise
¼ cup Heinz chili sauce
2 boiled eggs, chopped
2 tablespoons green bell pepper, chopped
2 tablespoons celery, chopped
2 tablespoons onion, finely chopped
1 teaspoon paprika
¼ teaspoon salt

Combine all ingredients and refrigerate for 2 hours. Serve over salads and/or seafood appetizers.

Serves 6 to 8

Bonita Favre

MOM'S SIDELINE SHRIMP SALAD

Shrimp boil, enough for 5 pounds of shrimp
5   pounds (50-60 count per pound) shrimp
6   hard boiled eggs, chopped
3   celery hearts, chopped
3   bunches green onions, snipped with kitchen shears
1   tablespoon dried parsley
1   tablespoon olive oil
2   teaspoons Tony Chachere's seasoning
1   cup mayonnaise
      Lettuce, enough to line serving bowl
      Tomato wedges

Boil shrimp in shrimp boil according to shrimp boil directions. Chop shrimp in bite size pieces. Combine remaining ingredients, except lettuce and tomatoes, and mix well. Refrigerate at least 1 hour before serving. Place in a lettuce lined serving bowl with tomato wedges. Serve with crackers.

Serves 12 to 14

Bonita Favre

AUNT FANNIE'S SQUASH SALAD

3   medium zucchini, julienne
3   medium yellow squash, julienne
2   medium ripe tomatoes, cut into wedges
1   bottle lemon dill dressing
1   cup plain yogurt
¼   cup lemon juice
½   teaspoon salt
1   teaspoon sugar
1   tablespoon dill (fresh or dried, but no seeds)

Combine zucchini, squash, tomatoes and lemon dill dressing, cover and chill for at least three hours. Stir vegetables or shake the container a couple of times. To serve, remove vegetables from the dressing. Combine the vegetable mixture and remaining ingredients in a one-pint jar or other water-tight container and shake until well blended.

Serves 6 to 8

Fannie Favre

37

MORGAN'S CAJUN POTATO SALAD

8 eggs
5 pounds potatoes, peeled and cut in large chunks
½ cup liquid crab boil
½ cup mayonnaise
3 tablespoons Creole mustard
¼ cup salt
Pepper to taste
Paprika

Boil eggs. In a separate pot, boil potatoes in crab boil for 20 minutes. Place potatoes in a large bowl. Peel eggs and extract yolks. Mix yolks with mayonnaise and mustard until creamy. Chop egg whites and place in bowl with potatoes. Add yolk mixture and blend well. Season with salt and pepper. Serve warm or chilled. Sprinkle with paprika.

Serves 12 to 14

Morgan Kowalski

Scott and Morgan

GRILLED CHICKEN SALAD

2 chicken breasts (or may substitute 5 pounds of shrimp, 50-60 count per pound)
1 green bell pepper, coarsely chopped
1 tomato, diced
1 cucumber, sliced
1 onion, coarsely chopped
2 boiled eggs, diced
Fresh mushrooms, sliced
Croutons
Lettuce or spinach leaves
Salt to taste
Pepper to taste
Parmesan cheese, grated
Your favorite salad dressing

Grill chicken breast and slice into ½ inch wide strips. Combine remaining ingredients, except Parmesan cheese, then place chicken on top, and sprinkle with Parmesan cheese.

Serves 6 to 8

Scott Favre

FRIED CRAWFISH SALAD

½   cup romaine lettuce, cut into bite size pieces
½   cup iceberg lettuce, cut into bite size pieces
2   pounds fried crawfish tails (refer to page 67)
2   ounces Parmesan cheese, shredded
    Dressing of choice
⅓   cup croutons
    Salt to taste
    Pepper to taste

Lay the romaine and iceberg lettuce on bottom of serving dish, then add crawfish. Sprinkle cheese over top of salad. Then pour the dressing on top of salad and place croutons on top. Then add salt and pepper.

Substitution: You can add boiled shrimp instead of crawfish tails.

Serves 6 to 8

Rhonda Favre

Rhonda enjoying crawfish.

SHRIMP & PASTA SALAD

4   hard boiled eggs, chopped
½   cup onions, chopped
¼   cup celery, chopped
½   cup black olives, chopped
½   cup dill pickles, chopped
2   cups shrimp, boiled
4   cups cooked elbow macaroni
1   cup mayonnaise
2   tablespoons olive oil
1   teaspoon lemon juice
2   teaspoons Worcestershire sauce
1   tablespoon mustard
½   cup ketchup
     Tabasco sauce to taste

In a large mixing bowl combine eggs, onions, celery, olives and pickles. Add shrimp and macaroni and toss lightly. In a small bowl, whisk together the remaining ingredients. Pour over mixture in large bowl and mix well. Cover and marinate for 2 hours.

Serves 6 to 8

Layne Bourgeois

FROSTED FRUIT SALAD

1   package lemon Jell-O
1   package orange Jell-O
2   cups hot water
1 ½ cups cold water
     Juice of 1 lemon
1   2-pound can crushed pineapple, drained (save juice)
2   bananas, sliced
10   marshmallows, diced

TOPPING

2   tablespoons flour
½   cup sugar
1   egg, slightly beaten
1   cup pineapple juice (drained from can)
2   tablespoons butter
1   cup whipped cream
½   cup grated sharp cheese or ½ cup nuts, chopped

Dissolve Jell-O in hot water. Add cold water. Chill until partially thickened. Put lemon juice over bananas and let stand for a few minutes. Fold in pineapple, bananas and marshmallows. Pour into 9x13 pan and chill until firm.

For topping, mix flour and sugar in a heavy pan. Add egg and pineapple juice. If there is not sufficient juice to make 1 cup, add water, cook, stirring constantly until thick. Add butter and cool. When cold, fold in whipped cream. Spread on gelatin and sprinkle with either cheese or nuts.

This may be made the day before, as lemon juice keeps bananas from turning dark.

Serves 6 to 8

Louise French Green

GUMBO, SOUPS AND SAUCES

With the first cool breezes of late fall and early winter in South Mississippi and the passing of the hot and humid temperatures, the locals begin to crave bowls of soups or stews. It's also gumbo season! Gumbo starts with a roux (recipe to follow) and cooked okra or filé to thicken. Filé is made from sassafras leaves, which derived from the Favre descendants, the Choctaw Indians. The Choctaw's word for sassafras is kombo - and this is where we get our word gumbo.

Smothered okra is cooked with the gumbo. Filé is added after the gumbo is cooked and put in just before serving. Beware, if filé is added while cooking, the gumbo becomes stringy. There are many variations to gumbos, soups and stews, as indicated in the recipes that follow in this chapter. There are no defined ingredients. You can use seafood alone, or combine with meats, sausage, chicken or game. Whatever the results they are sure to be delicious!

The Favres are also known for some very interesting soup concoctions. Our maternal great-grandmother, Nono, made a Poor Man's Soup. This was a combination of any and all ingredients that happened to be available, which basically, was a clear version of vegetable soup. It's O.K. to jump right in. I guess every season can be gumbo season!

Bonita Favre

Pass Bait Shop

What better place to tell the story of your day's catch than the place where you bought the bait.

Only true tales are allowed to be shared here, and there is no reason to believe that that directive has ever been violated. At least no one there has ever admitted to a lie. Norman, Bruce, Barbara, Robbie, Pam. Ask them. They'll tell you.

ROUX

Making a roux can be very sensitive. The best pot or skillet to use is a black iron or heavy cast iron skillet. If you burn it, you just as well throw it away and start over again. Make sure you clean the pot or skillet well. I like my roux a little lighter than the color of an old copper penny. As you make it more often, you will figure out whether you like yours dark or light. The roux generally takes around an hour before it reaches the color I like. I prefer my roux on the thin side, meaning less flour, but you can add more flour for a thicker consistency. It can be used for stews, soups, gumbos, sauce piquants, gravies, sauces, etouffees and more.

1   cup oil of your choice
2   cups white flour

Heat oil in skillet. Add in flour slowly. Cook on medium to low heat for 1 hour. As the roux starts to turn dark be sure to stir it with a whisk making a figure 8 motion. Be sure not to let it burn!

Jeff Favre

GENERAL STOCK

1   pound meat of your choice (crawfish, chicken, shrimp, fish, seafood etc.)
½   quart water
3   stems parsley
½   onion, chopped
½   teaspoon pepper
½   teaspoon salt
½   teaspoon hot sauce

Boil all ingredients for 1 hour. Let cool, then strain. Keep chilled or frozen, until ready for use.

Yields 1 quart

Jeff Favre

LEMON BUTTER SAUCE

½   pound butter
1   teaspoon Worcestershire sauce
1   tablespoon lemon juice
1   teaspoon salt
1   teaspoon Tony Chachere's seasoning
1   tablespoon fresh parsley

Over low heat in small saucepan or skillet, melt butter and add remaining ingredients, mixing well

Use as a baste over fish, gator or chicken.

Yields 1 cup

Jeff Favre

CREOLE MARINADE

1 cup Worchestershire sauce
½ cup butter
2 cups Crystal hot sauce
1 teaspoon salt
1 teaspoon pepper
1 teaspoon Tony Chachere's seasonings
1 teaspoon garlic salt

Combine all ingredients. Use on turkey, chicken, etc.

Yields 2 ½ cups

Jeff Favre

Jeff injecting a turkey with Creole marinade.

COCKTAIL SAUCE

1   8-ounce bottle chili sauce
4   tablespoons horseradish or to taste (we like it spicy)
1   teaspoon lemon juice
1   tablespoon Worcestershire sauce
2   tablespoons parsley
1   teaspoon Tabasco sauce
1   tablespoon olive oil

Mix all ingredients well and chill. Serve with shrimp.

Serves 6 to 8

Scott Favre

WHITE GRAVY

2   tablespoons butter
2   tablespoons all-purpose flour
¼   teaspoon salt
     Dash of white pepper
1   cup milk

Melt butter in saucepan over low heat. Blend in flour, salt and white pepper.

Add milk all at once. Cook quickly, stirring constantly, until mixture thickens and bubbles.

Remove from heat when it bubbles. At this point, you can add cheese or other flavorings.

Serve over biscuits, chicken or country fried steak.

Serves 4 to 6

Bonita Favre

TARTAR SAUCE

3	cups Hellman's mayonnaise
1	cup pickle relish
1	tablespoon Worcestershire sauce
1	teaspoon Tabasco sauce
½	cup green onions, finely chopped
1	tablespoon parsley, fresh preferred
	Tony Chachere's seasoning to taste
	Salt to taste

Combine all ingredients and mix well. Refrigerate and serve with fried seafood, it's especially good with catfish.

Serves 6 to 8

Jeff Favre

CRAWFISH & CORN SOUP

½	cup onion, chopped
½	cup green onions, chopped
½	cup green bell pepper, chopped
2	cloves of garlic, minced
1	pound pre-cooked crawfish tails (may substitute 1 pound of blue crab with claws)
2	cans cream corn
1	cup half & half
1	teaspoon salt
1	teaspoon pepper
1	tablespoon liquid crab boil
	Tabasco sauce to taste
	Dash of parsley

Sauté onion, green onions, bell pepper and garlic until tender. Add crawfish, corn, and half & half. Bring to a boil. Reduce heat and add remaining ingredients. Cook until soup thickens. Serve.

Serves 4 to 6

Irvin Favre

AUNT SHUG'S JEZEBEL SAUCE

Delicious with pork or roast beef.

1   18-ounce jar pineapple preserves
1   18-ounce jar apple jelly
1   ounce dry mustard
1   5-ounce jar horseradish
1   tablespoon cracked pepper

Combine all ingredients, blend well. Put in jelly jars and refrigerate. Will keep 3 to 6 months.

Serves 6 to 8

Irma Mallini

Bonita and Irma

OYSTER SOUP

3   dozen oysters
½   stick butter
1   small onion, chopped
½   cup green bell pepper, chopped
½   stalk celery, chopped
2   cloves garlic, minced
½   cup green onion, chopped
1   teaspoon salt
      Dash of cayenne pepper
1   teaspoon pepper
1   quart milk
1   sprig fresh parsley, chopped

Drain oysters and set them aside. In butter, sauté the onion, pepper, celery, garlic and one-half of the allowed green onions until tender. Add oysters, remaining green onions, salt, cayenne and pepper. Add milk slowly and heat rapidly. Just before milk comes to a boil, remove from heat and stir. Add chopped parsley to garnish and serve.

Serves 6 to 8

Jeff Favre

VEGETABLE BEEF SOUP

2   pounds cubed chuck roast
8   cups water
2   carrots, sliced
1   green bell pepper, chopped
5   stalks celery, chopped
1   can crushed tomatoes
1   potato, cubed
1   teaspoon sugar
1   teaspoon salt
1   teaspoon pepper

Boil meat in water until tender. Remove meat from broth. Add carrots, bell pepper, celery, tomatoes, potato and sugar. Simmer until vegetables are tender. Return meat to pot and season with salt and pepper. Heat thoroughly and serve.

Serves 6 to 8

Izella French

HOT & SPICY VEGETABLE BEEF SOUP

Great meal with a salad and some cornbread.

1   pound ground chuck
46   ounces Hot and Spicy V-8 juice
1   envelope dry onion soup mix
1   tablespoon sugar
1   package frozen gumbo mix or soup veggies
     Tony Chachere's seasoning to taste
     Salt (if needed)
     Cheddar cheese, grated

Brown ground chuck and drain. Put all other ingredients, except cheese, in stock pot and boil until okra in frozen gumbo mix is tender. Add ground chuck to mixture and simmer for 25 minutes. Sprinkle with Cheddar cheese after each serving is ladled into bowls.

(Try cabbage and red beans instead of vegetables, for a different taste.)

Serves 6 to 8

Judy Pursell

CHICKEN SOUP

1   small fryer, skinned and cut up
     Salt to taste
     Pepper to taste
5   quarts water
1   tablespoon liquid crab boil
1   onion, finely chopped
4   cloves garlic, finely chopped
3   stalks celery, chopped
½   green bell pepper, finely chopped
2   medium potatoes, diced
3   carrots, diced
6   ounces pasta of your choice
¼   cup chopped parsley

Wash, drain and season chicken with salt and pepper. In a large stock pot, add water, crab boil and boil chicken with onion, garlic, celery and bell pepper until chicken is tender. Remove chicken from pot and let cool. Skim fat from soup. Add potatoes, carrots and pasta. Debone chicken and return to soup. Add parsley and cook until potatoes and carrots are tender.

Serves 10 to 12

Izella French

SEAFOOD GUMBO

¾   cup vegetable oil
¾   cup all-purpose flour
2   cups onions, chopped
2   cups green bell peppers, chopped
1   cup celery, chopped
2   tablespoons garlic, minced
2   bay leaves
    Dash of salt
    Dash of pepper
    Dash of oregano
1   teaspoon thyme
5   cups basic seafood stock (see page 43)
1   pound smoked sausage, sliced
1   pound (30-40 count per pound) shrimp, peeled
1   pint oysters and liquor
1   pound crabmeat
    Mushrooms (optional)
3   cups cooked rice

Heat vegetable oil in large skillet over high heat for about 4-5 minutes until hot. Gradually add flour, whisking constantly. Continue cooking until dark brown, about 3-4 minutes. Immediately add onions, bell peppers and celery, stirring well. Cook for 2 minutes. Add garlic, bay leaves, salt, pepper, oregano and thyme and stir another minute. Add stock slowly while stirring until all is added. Bring to a boil and add sausage. Continue to boil for 5 minutes. Reduce heat and add shrimp, oysters, crabmeat and mushrooms. Let simmer for 10 minutes.

Serve with rice. Take out bay leaves before serving.

Serves 10 to 12

Bonita Favre

OYSTER ARTICHOKE SOUP

¼   cup olive oil
½   cup green onions, chopped
½   cup parsley
1   cup artichoke puree
3   cups oyster liquor or vegetable stock
1   tablespoon garlic, minced
1   cup whipping cream
2   dozen oysters and their liquor
     Tabasco sauce to taste
     Salt to taste
     Pepper to taste

Sauté onions and parsley in olive oil, until clear. Add pureed artichoke and stock, mix well, then add garlic. Add in whipping cream,
cover, reduce heat and simmer for 30 minutes. Add oysters and
liquor, then stir. Turn off heat. Season with Tabasco sauce, salt and
pepper. Serve when oysters curl.

Serves 4 to 6

Scott Favre

Bonita Favre earned her master's degree in education while raising four children and working. Sometimes Scott, Brett, Jeff and Brandi would have to go along with Bonita and play some type of sports outside her classroom.

CRAWFISH BISQUE

4	tablespoons margarine or butter
4	tablespoons flour
1	onion, chopped
1	rib celery, chopped
2	cloves garlic, minced
1	6-ounce can tomato paste
1	teaspoon sugar
1	pound pre-cooked crawfish tails
2	quarts warm water
	Salt to taste
	Pepper to taste
2	cups rice
¼	cup green onions, chopped
¼	cup parsley, chopped

Make a light roux (see page 43) with butter and flour in Dutch oven. Remove from heat and add onion, celery, and garlic. Stir in tomato paste, sugar and crawfish. Sauté for 5 minutes. Add warm water and bring to a boil. Reduce heat and simmer for 15 minutes. Add salt and pepper. Serve over rice with green onions and parsley.

Serves 6 to 8

Scott Favre

CAJUN CHOWDER

1   Spanish onion, finely diced
2   carrots, peeled and finely diced
3   stalks celery, finely diced
1   each green, yellow and red bell pepper, finely diced
1   tablespoon garlic, chopped
3   tablespoons olive oil
12   ounces cream sherry
2-4 strips cooked bacon, crumbled
2   tomatoes, chopped
3   cooked potatoes, peeled and diced
2   small cans clams, chopped
16   ounces clam juice
8   ounces chicken broth
8   ounces crawfish tail meat
2   tablespoons chicken paste
8   ounces tomato paste
3   cups water
2   tablespoons parsley, chopped
1   tablespoon chives, chopped
    White pepper to taste
    Salt to taste
    Cayenne pepper to taste
1   tablespoon basil
1   tablespoon oregano
1   tablespoon Cajun seasoning
3   cups cream
    Corn starch to thicken

Sauté onion, carrots, celery, peppers and garlic in olive oil for 5 minutes, or until they sweat. Add sherry and reduce until almost gone. Add cooked bacon, tomatoes and potatoes. Add clams, clam juice, chicken broth, crawfish tail meat, chicken paste, tomato paste and water.

Add all spices and let simmer 1 hour. Add cream and continue to simmer 30 minutes. Thicken with cornstarch and water until semi-thick (it should coat back of spoon). Taste to check seasonings; add more to your taste.

Serves 10 to 12

Chef Channing Boyer
Green Bay, WI

BRETT FAVRE'S
STEAKHOUSE

DAD'S SPICY CORN STEW

1	green bell pepper, finely chopped
1	white onion, finely chopped
1	clove garlic, minced
¼	cup cooking oil
2	sausage links, sliced
1	can Rotel tomatoes
4	cans cream corn
2	cups cooked rice

Sauté bell pepper, onion and garlic in a 2-quart pot with cooking oil. Cook for 20 minutes on medium heat, then add sausage. Cook for 10 minutes. Add Rotel tomatoes and cook for 5 minutes. Then add cream corn and cook all ingredients for 20 minutes. Serve over rice.

Serves 4 to 6

Irvin Favre

BIG IRV'S CORN STEW

Growing up around the Favre house was always exciting when it came to the dinner table. No matter what meal hit the table you could always expect plenty to eat. As kids, though, we would never know what to expect. We could be eating anything from black-eyed peas with Meemaw's pig ass and cabbage (cabbage with ham) to Big Irv's famous corn stew. He prepared corn stew more than any other meal. Thanks to Brett's new found friends people as far away as Wisconsin now have Big Irv's recipe. Corn stew can be prepared very quickly and it is great eating. The only thing you have to watch out for is the spice. Sometimes Big Irv goes a little overboard with the spice. It is always important to be prepared with a wet cloth with an ice cube to cool the lips.

Jeff Favre

Big Irv

AUNT IRMA'S CHICKEN & OYSTER GUMBO

1	3 to 4 pound hen, cut into pieces
	Salt to taste
	Cayenne pepper to taste
	Pepper to taste
2	bay leaves
½	teaspoon thyme
1	pint oysters with their liquid
1	cup cooking oil
1	cup flour
2	bunch green onions, chopped
½	bunch fresh parsley
½	teaspoon poultry seasoning
10	cups chicken broth
1	teaspoon filé
2	cups cooked rice

Season chicken with salt, cayenne and pepper. Boil chicken with bay leaves and thyme until done. In another pan simmer oysters in their liquid, just until curled. In a heavy black iron pot, make a dark roux (see page 43) with the oil and flour, stirring constantly. When the roux is brown, add the green onions and parsley. Cook until wilted. Add poultry seasoning, chicken broth and deboned chicken. Add the oysters and liquid and cook for 1 hour on low to medium heat. If the gumbo becomes too thick, simply add more broth. Add filé and serve over rice.

Serves 8 to 10

Irma J. Mallini (Ricka)

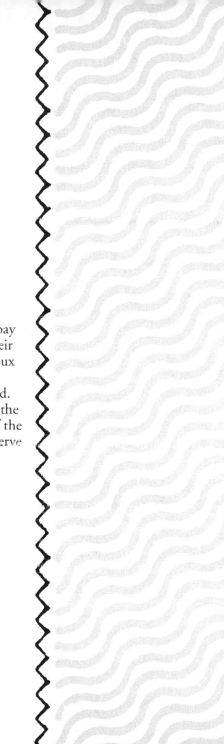

MEXICAN SOUP

4	slices bacon, diced
¾	cup onions, sliced
¾	cup celery, chopped
½	cup green pepper, chopped
1	clove garlic, minced
1	16-ounce can refried beans
½	teaspoon pepper
½	teaspoon chili powder
	Dash Tabasco sauce
1	14-ounce can chicken broth
1	cup Cheddar cheese, shredded
	Tomatoes, chopped, to taste
	Tortilla chips, crushed, to taste

In 2-quart saucepan, cook bacon until crisp. Add onions, celery, green pepper and garlic. Cook, covered, over low heat, stirring occasionally, about 10 minutes, or until vegetables are tender but not brown. Add beans, pepper, chili powder and Tabasco. Stir in chicken broth. Bring to boil.

Serve in bowls and sprinkle with tomatoes, cheese and tortilla chips.

Serves 6 to 8

Krissy Wittmann Vincent

AUNT FANNIE'S HAM BONE SOUP

One whole ham bone (buy a fully cooked ham, it's okay to leave some ham on the bone.)

Lots of vegetables - potatoes, carrots, onions, cabbage, cauliflower, green beans, Brussels sprouts, whatever you have on hand. Canned things are okay, but fresh is much better.

Garlic is the only seasoning I use in this soup, but that is up to you.

Cover the ham bone with water in a large pot. Boil the ham bone for at least 45 minutes before adding anything else. Then add the vegetables in order of cooking time—potatoes and carrots take longer so they go first.

The ham will make the soup salty enough for most so do not add salt while you are cooking. Serve over corn bread.

Fannie Favre

MEEMAW'S SPLIT PEA SOUP

1	pound dried split peas
2	pounds smoked sausage, sliced into ½ inch pieces
6	carrots, diced
2	medium onions, chopped
4	cloves garlic, chopped
1	celery stalk, chopped
1	green bell pepper, chopped
½	pound bacon, fried, cut into pieces, save drippings
	Salt to taste
	Pepper to taste
	Tony Chachere's seasoning to taste

Wash peas and put in a large pot filled with enough water to cover peas. Add sliced sausage, carrots, onions, garlic, celery and bell pepper. Add bacon to pot of peas, along with the drippings from the bacon. Cook on low heat until peas are cooked to a mush. Add water as needed. Season with salt, pepper and Tony Chachere's.

Serves 6 to 8

Meemaw (Izella) French

MEEMAW'S CHICKEN & OKRA GUMBO

18 chicken thighs
2   pounds cut okra, frozen
1   10 ½-ounce can tomatoes, mashed
2   large onions, chopped
4   tablespoons flour
4   tablespoons cooking oil
1   celery stalk, chopped
    Dash of cumin
5   cloves garlic, chopped
    Salt to taste
    Dash of lemon pepper
    Tony Chachere's seasoning to taste

To make stock, skin chicken thighs, and put in large pot, covered with water. Cook over medium heat. In a frying pan, coated with cooking oil, fry okra until it is not slimy, then add tomatoes and onions. Make roux (see page 43) with the flour and oil to desired color. Add celery, cumin and garlic. Add okra, tomatoes and roux to the chicken and cook until chicken is done. Add salt, lemon pepper and Tony Chachere's.

Serves 8 to 10

Meemaw (Izella) French

Brett, Bonita, Jade and Meemaw enjoying the outdoors.

MAWMAW FAVRE'S RED GRAVY STEW

3   pounds beef chuck roast
½   cup flour
⅓   cup cooking oil
2   cups onions, chopped
2   stalks celery, chopped
2   cups hot water
1   bay leaf
1   10-ounce Rotel diced tomatoes and green chiles
1   28-ounce can Hunt's whole tomatoes
1   15-ounce Hunt's tomato sauce
6   potatoes, pared and quartered
2   15-ounce cans sliced carrots
1   teaspoon sugar
    Salt to taste
    Pepper to taste
2   cups cooked rice

Cut roast into bite size pieces. Dredge in flour. Brown meat in cooking oil over medium heat. Remove meat from pot as it browns. When all meat is browned, pour left over flour in remaining oil and stir about 10 minutes. Add onions, celery, hot water, bay leaf and stir until mixed. Add Rotel, tomatoes, tomato sauce, potatoes, carrots and sugar. Return meat to pot and simmer for 1 to 1 ½ hours or until meat is tender. Season with salt and pepper before serving. Serve over rice.

Serves 8 to 10

Mary Favre

RED BEANS & SAUSAGE SOUP

Note: You may need to add more water if soup gets too thick or the beans aren't tender.

2	tablespoons oil
3	tablespoons fresh garlic, minced
3	tablespoons shallots or yellow onion, minced
2	pounds dry red beans
3 ½	quarts cold water
2	tablespoons chicken base
1	tablespoon chili powder
1	tablespoon cumin
1	teaspoon Cajun seasoning (add more if you want it spicy)
	Salt to taste
	Pepper to taste
1	pound andouille sausage, sliced into ½ pieces, or any other pre-cooked sausage
2	cups cooked white rice
1	cup red, yellow and green peppers, diced

Heat an 8 ½-quart heavy sauce pan on medium high heat. Add in oil, garlic and shallots. Sauté until tender, but not brown. Stir in red beans and add water. Bring to a boil and then reduce heat to simmer. Add in chicken base and dry spices. Stir well and simmer for approximately 1 hour, or until beans are tender and soup is thick. Stir often so the beans don't burn on the bottom of the pan. Add sausage to soup; simmer an extra 10 to 15 minutes. To serve, garnish the top of the soup with rice and peppers.

Serves 10 to 12

Chef Dean McArthur
Milwaukee, WI

BEEF STEW

2   pounds beef chuck roast, cut into bite size pieces
¼   cup cooking oil
1   onion, chopped
2   stalks celery, chopped
1   clove garlic, minced
1   bay leaf
2 ¼   cups water
1   tablespoon salt
1   teaspoon pepper
4   potatoes, peeled and quartered
6   carrots, peeled and quartered
2   tablespoons all-purpose flour
1   teaspoon sugar
2   cups cooked rice

In a Dutch oven, brown meat in cooking oil, turning often. Remove meat from pot and add onion, celery, garlic and bay leaf with 2 cups of water. Add salt, pepper and replace meat. Simmer for 1 ½ hours, stirring occasionally. Add potatoes and carrots. Cover and cook 30 to 45 minutes or until vegetables are tender. Skim the fat from liquid. Take 1 ¾ cups of liquid and combine with ¼ cup water and 2 tablespoons all-purpose flour until smooth. Slowly stir into hot liquid. Add sugar. Cook and stir about 3 minutes. Remove bay leaf. Serve over rice.

Serves 8 to 10

Bonita Favre

Some of the best food I have ever eaten has been at the Favre residence. At age 14, when Brett and I began courting, I was very shy about eating around the family. Therefore, I was always the last in line. I learned very quickly that in the Favre house "First come, first served" meant there may not be any left for the last in line. Ultimately, this decision to be last soon changed. I became first in line when the dinner bell rang.

Deanna Favre

Deanna
and Brett on their way
to the Junior - Senior Prom.

BRETT, DEANNA & BRITTANY FAVRE FAMILY CHILI

½	cup green onions, chopped
2	green bell peppers, diced
2	celery stalks, chopped
1	small onion, chopped
2	cloves garlic, minced
4	tablespoons butter
1 ½	pounds ground beef
	Salt to taste
	Pepper to taste
	Tony Chachere's seasoning to taste
	Chili powder to taste
1	package McCormick chili seasoning
1	8-ounce can Hunt's diced tomatoes
1	8-ounce can Hunt's diced roasted garlic tomatoes
1	8-ounce can Rotel diced tomatoes and green chilies
1	8-ounce can cream of mushroom soup
1	can kidney beans

Sauté green onions, peppers, celery, onion and garlic in butter. Brown ground beef with salt, pepper, Tony's Chachere's and chili powder. Drain. Combine meat with vegetables. Stir and simmer 10 minutes.

Stir in chili seasoning packet. Add canned tomatoes, cream of mushroom soup and kidney beans. Bring to a boil and reduce heat, cover and simmer about 30 minutes.

Optional: Serve fresh with green onions, jalapeno peppers, grated cheddar cheese and/or corn chips as Frito pie.

Serves 6 to 8

Brett, Deanna and Brittany Favre

My favorite foods:
Shrimp Creole, Hamburger Steak, Spaghetti and Meatballs, Red Beans and Sausage, Golette, Ham Rolls, Shrimp Dip

Deanna Favre

RICKA'S OYSTER STEW

2 or 3   dozen small oysters with liquid
6   green onions, finely chopped
1   stalk celery, finely chopped
1   quart milk
1   stick butter
    Salt to taste
    Pepper to taste
    Worcestershire sauce
    Tabasco sauce to taste

Strain oysters and save liquid. Be sure to pick shells off oysters. Cook green onions, celery and oysters in their liquid until they are plump and edges begin to curl. While oysters are cooking, simmer milk and butter in saucepan. DO NOT BOIL. Add oyster mixture to milk and butter. Simmer a few minutes. Add salt, pepper, Worcestershire and Tabasco.

Serves 6 to 8

Irma Mallini

CHICKEN ZUCCHINI MUSHROOM SOUP

This makes an excellent light soup appetizer.

1   large onion, chopped
1   large green bell pepper, chopped
2   pounds deboned chicken, cubed
2   quarts water
4   cubes chicken bouillon
3   medium sized zucchini, chopped
½   pound fresh mushrooms, sliced
1   teaspoon garlic powder
    Salt to taste
    Pepper to taste

Boil onion, bell pepper and chicken in water with bouillon for ½ hour. Add zucchini and mushrooms. Add garlic powder, salt and pepper and cook an additional ½ hour.

Serves 6

Leslie Talley

LESLIE'S POTATO SOUP

10-12	medium size potatoes, cubed
1	large onion, chopped
1	tablespoon salt
1	teaspoon pepper
1	teaspoon Tony Chachere's seasoning
1	teaspoon garlic, minced or garlic powder
1	ham bone or salt meat
3	tablespoons butter
2	gallons cold water
1	8-ounce half & half (optional)
½	cup instant mashed potatoes (optional)
	Shredded cheese (optional)
	Sour cream (optional)
	Bacon bits (optional)

Add potatoes, onion, salt, pepper, Tony's, garlic, meat or ham bone and butter to a pot of 2 gallons cold water. Cook on medium to high heat for 25-30 minutes or until potatoes begin to crumble. Add half & half and instant mashed potatoes for desired texture (creamy and thickness). Cook for an additional 5 minutes. Serve with toppings (shredded cheese, sour cream and bacon bits).

Serves 6 to 8

Leslie Ladner

SEAFOOD AND FISH

For as long as I can remember, seafood has always been a mainstay of the Favre family. Around our house, we were always having boiled shrimp, crabs or crawfish and other seafood dishes.

When we first thought about writing a cookbook, seafood dishes were the first thing that came to mind. Our entire family loves seafood and there is always some type of seafood available, whether it is fried speckled-trout caught fresh from the Gulf or a sack of boiled crawfish spread over the picnic table in the spring. More than half of the meals we eat are seafood, so naturally this is our favorite section of the cookbook. Each family member has their own favorite dish. Whether it is Meemaw's Shrimp Creole, Mom's Marinated Crabs or Brett's Crawfish Etouffee. Everybody here on the Coast loves seafood. I think you will enjoy the recipes in this section. They are sure to awaken your taste buds. Get ready for some unforgettable dining experiences.

Scott Favre

For those of you who do not have access to fresh seafood here are a couple of phone numbers for ordering seafood. And it will be delivered to your front door.

C.F. Gallott & Son Seafood, Inc.
Dentral Avenue
D'Iberville, MS 39532
Phone (228) 392-2719
Fax (228) 392-8848

Open 9 a.m. to 5:30 p.m. CST

Louisiana Pride & Seafood
4418 Downman Road
New Orleans, LA 70126
Phone (800) 884-2607
Phone (504) 245-1661

Open Monday - Saturday
9 a.m. - 5 p.m. CST

Shrimp comes in many sizes. The way we distinguish between sizes is by the number of shrimp per pound. Our recipes will be using this method. An example is Easy Barbecued Shrimp, which calls for 2 pounds (15-20 count per pound) shrimp. The recipe calls for 2 pounds of shrimp that are large enough to only have 15 to 20 shrimp per pound. Size of shrimp is recommended only. You may vary from this as needed.

Opening Day

Each year the opening of shrimp season produces a lot of activity in the coastal harbors.

Boats have to change their rigging from the dredges of the just-ended oyster season to the nets used for shrimping.

There's nothing easy about this way of life. The engines have been tuned. The boats have been rigged. Now they wait for the word to go. The shrimp have to be a certain size before harvesting. But how plentiful will they be? There's no sure way to tell.

So it goes season after season.

GAMBINO'S BOILED CRAWFISH

10	gallons water
½	gallon liquid crab boil
1	26-ounce box of salt
¼	cup cayenne pepper
2	32-ounce box of powdered crab boil
1	small bag lemons
1	5-pound bag potatoes (approximately 10 - 12)
5	cloves garlic
1	head celery, cut in half
10	onions, cut in half
1	40-pound sack of crawfish, cleaned well

Bring to a boil 10 gallons of water with all ingredients except crawfish. Add crawfish and bring to a boil again. Cook 10-12 minutes, then let crawfish soak an additional 15 minutes. Crawfish are juicy and ready to serve. (The longer the crawfish soak the hotter they will get.)

Shrimp (40 pounds)...2 minutes boiling, 15 minutes soaking.
Crabs (6 dozens)...5-7 minutes boiling, 15 minutes soaking.

Note: Adjust seasoning accordingly for more or less seafood.

Serves 12 to 14

Mark Gambino

Mark Gambino
master crawfish chef.

FRIED CRAWFISH TAILS

1   egg
1   cup milk
2   tablespoons onion powder
2   tablespoons garlic powder
½   teaspoon salt
½   teaspoon pepper
1   pound pre-cooked crawfish tails
      Zatarain's fish fry
      Frying oil

In a large bowl, mix egg, milk, onion powder, garlic powder, salt and pepper. Dip crawfish into egg mixture. Remove from egg mixture and dip each crawfish tail into fish fry and deep fry in oil until golden brown.

Serves 4 to 6

Rhonda Favre

CRAWFISH CAKES

1   pound pre-cooked crawfish tails
1   onion, chopped
1   green bell pepper, chopped
2   cloves garlic, minced
½   stick butter
2   eggs
1   cup bread crumbs
      Salt to taste
      Pepper to taste
      Flour
      Frying Oil

Sauté crawfish tails, onion, bell pepper and garlic in butter for 2 minutes. Combine with eggs and bread crumbs. Add salt and pepper. Shape into cakes and sprinkle with flour. Deep fry in oil or panee until golden brown.

Serves 4 to 6

Scott Favre

BRETT, DEANNA & BRITTANY FAVRE FAMILY ETOUFFEE

2	green bell peppers, chopped
3	stalks celery, chopped
½	cup green onions, chopped
1	onion, chopped
3	cloves garlic
1	stick butter
3	cans cream of mushroom soup
2	8-ounce cans Rotel diced tomatoes
1	pound pre-cooked crawfish tails, peeled
	Tony Chachere's seasoning to taste
	Salt to taste
	Pepper to taste
2	cups cooked rice

Sauté bell peppers, celery, green onions, onion and garlic in butter. Add cream of mushroom soup and stir until smooth. Add Rotel tomatoes until mixed well. Add in Tony Chachere's, salt and pepper. Simmer 10 minutes, then add crawfish tails and bring to a boil. Simmer about 30 minutes. Serve over rice. Also great served with garlic bread.

Serves 6 to 8

Brett, Deanna and Brittany Favre

Brett, Brittany and Deanna

(Photo by Turba Photography)

CRAWFISH STEW

½   cup flour
½   cup butter
1   green bell pepper, chopped
1   onion, chopped
2   cloves garlic, chopped
1   stalk celery, chopped
1   pound pre-cooked crawfish tails
½   teaspoon salt
½   teaspoon pepper
    Water or seafood stock
¼   cup green onions, chopped
¼   cup parsley
2   cups cooked rice

Make roux (see page 43) with flour and butter. When roux is dark brown, remove from heat and add bell pepper, onion, garlic and celery. Stir for 3-4 minutes. Add crawfish tails, salt, pepper and water or seafood stock to cover all ingredients. Simmer for 30 minutes. Add green onions and parsley. Serve over rice.

Serves 6 to 8

Scott Favre

CRAWFISH & PASTA

1	onion, chopped
2	cloves garlic, minced
1	green bell pepper, chopped
½	cup green onions, chopped
¼	cup butter
2	tablespoons flour
¼	cup parsley
1	pound pre-cooked crawfish tails
¼	pound Velveeta cheese
½	cup Parmesan cheese
1	pint half & half
	Salt to taste
	Pepper to taste
½	pound fettucine

Sauté onion, garlic, bell pepper and green onions in butter until tender. Add flour, parsley and crawfish tails. Cook for 15 minutes. Add Velveeta and Parmesan cheeses and half & half. Reduce heat and simmer for 10 minutes. Stir to prevent sticking. Season with salt and pepper. Cook pasta and drain. Add to crawfish mixture and serve with garlic bread.

Serves 6 to 8

Scott Favre

WOODY'S CRAWFISH PIE

1   onion, chopped
1   green bell pepper, chopped
1   stalk celery, chopped
2   cloves garlic, minced
½   cup green onions, chopped
½   cup butter
¼   cup flour
1   pound pre-cooked crawfish tails
1 ½ cup heavy cream
¼   cup parsley
½   teaspoon salt
½   teaspoon pepper
1   9-inch pie shell and top, unbaked

Sauté onion, bell pepper, celery, garlic and green onions in butter until tender. Add flour and crawfish tails and cook for 10 minutes. Add cream and parsley and cook for 5 minutes. Add salt and pepper. Pour mixture into pie shell and cover with top of crust. Pinch edges and punch holes in the top to vent. Bake 1 hour at 350° F, until crust is golden brown.

Serves 6 to 8

Destin "Woody" Brady

Even a power outage from Hurricane Georges didn't stop Destin from cooking.

71

Soft shell crabs are blue crabs that shed their shells to grow. They are commonly called "Buster crabs." They can be purchased at the store cleaned and ready to cook.

You may also find them fresh and uncleaned. If so it is necessary to prepare them for cooking by removing their eyes and their "Dead-man fingers" (lungs).

FRIED SOFT SHELL CRAB

1	egg
1	cup milk
1	tablespoon lemon juice
1	teaspoon salt
1	teaspoon pepper
½	dozen soft shell crabs
	Flour
	Zatarain's fish fry
	Frying oil

In a large bowl, mix egg, milk, lemon juice, salt and pepper. Soak crabs in egg mixture. Mix fish fry and flour in a 3-to-1 ratio and roll crabs in mixture. Deep fry in oil until golden brown.

Serves 4 to 6

Kendall Michel

CRABMEAT AU GRATIN

1   onion, chopped
1   green bell pepper, chopped
½   cup green onions, chopped
½   cup butter
4   tablespoons flour
1   pound lump crabmeat
1   teaspoon salt
1   teaspoon pepper
1   egg yolk
1   12-ounce can evaporated milk
1   cup shredded Cheddar cheese

Sauté onion, bell pepper, and green onions in butter until tender. Add flour and mix well. Remove from heat and add crabmeat, salt and pepper, egg yolk, milk and ½ cup of cheese. Pour in square casserole dish coated with cooking spray. Top with remaining cheese. Bake at 350° F for 20 minutes.

Serves 4 to 6

Scott Favre

GULF COAST CRAB CAKES

2   eggs
2   tablespoons mayonnaise
1   tablespoon Creole mustard
¼   cup minced onion
¼   cup minced green bell pepper
¼   cup green onions, chopped
1   pound crabmeat (claw or lump)
½   teaspoon salt
½   teaspoon pepper
1   cup bread crumbs
     Frying oil

Mix together eggs, mayonnaise, mustard, onion, bell pepper and green onions. Add in crabmeat, salt and pepper. Shape into round cakes and coat with bread crumbs. In a heavy skillet, fry each crab cake in enough oil to coat bottom of pan, until golden brown.

Serves 4 to 6

FAVRE FAMILY FAVORITE

SHRIMP & CRABMEAT AU GRATIN

Great with a fruit salad and good old crusty French bread.

2	white or yellow onions, finely chopped
4	green onions, finely chopped
1	stalk of celery, finely chopped
8	tablespoons butter
2	pounds (30-40 count per pound) shrimp, peeled and deveined
1	pound lump white crabmeat
1	can cream of mushroom soup
1	can mushrooms stem and pieces
½	cup fresh parsley, finely chopped
1	cup American cheese, grated
½	cup white wine
¾ - 1	cup buttered bread crumbs

Sauté onions, green onions and celery in butter until soft. Add shrimp; cook until pink. Add crabmeat, soup and mushrooms. When well blended, add parsley, cheese and white wine, heat thoroughly, but don't cook. Pour into a greased casserole or au gratin dishes. Sprinkle with buttered bread crumbs and bake at 400° F for about 20 minutes or until bread crumbs are browned.

Serves 6 to 8

Judy Pursell

CRABMEAT SCOOTER

½   cup green onions, chopped
½   cup parsley
2   tablespoons butter
2   tablespoons of flour
1   pint whipping cream
½   cup Parmesan cheese, grated
1   pound crabmeat
    Salt to taste
    Pepper to taste
    Pasta of your choice

Sauté onions and parsley in butter for 2 minutes. Add in flour, whipping cream and cheese. Stir until cheese melts. Add crabmeat, salt and pepper. Serve over pasta.

Serves 4 to 6

Scott Favre

MARINATED BOILED CRABS

8   ounces Italian dressing
3   tablespoons Worcestershire sauce
2   lemons, squeezed
1   teaspoon Creole mustard
1   teaspoon horseradish sauce
1   dozen boiled crabs, cleaned and cracked claws
2   stalks celery, chopped
1   onion, chopped
1   green bell pepper, chopped
2   cloves garlic, chopped

Mix Italian dressing, Worcestershire sauce, lemon juice, mustard and horseradish sauce. Pour mixture over crabs. Add in celery, onion, bell pepper and garlic. Marinate 1 day in a covered container in refrigerator, stirring occasionally.

Serves 8 to 10

Bonita Favre

CRABMEAT IMPERIAL

1   green bell pepper, chopped
2   pimentos, diced
1   tablespoon Creole mustard
2   eggs, beaten
1   cup mayonnaise
1   teaspoon salt
1   teaspoon pepper
2   pounds lump crabmeat

Mix together bell pepper, pimentos, mustard, eggs, mayonnaise, salt and pepper. Fold in crabmeat gently. Pour into a casserole dish coated with cooking spray. Bake at 350° F for 15 minutes.

Serves 4 to 6

Scott Favre

EASY BARBECUED SHRIMP

2   pounds (15 to 20 count per pound) shrimp, peeled
2   sticks butter
1   tablespoon cayenne pepper
¼   cup Worcestershire sauce
2   tablespoons garlic powder
1   tablespoon oregano
2   tablespoons parsley
¼   cup barbecue sauce
2   tablespoons lemon juice
2   tablespoons salt

Place shrimp in casserole dish. In a bowl, melt butter and mix remaining ingredients together. Pour over shrimp and bake at 350° F for 15-20 minutes. Serve with French bread.

Serves 4 to 6

Mark Gambino

FLOUNDER'S FRIED SHRIMP

2   eggs
1   cup milk
1   tablespoon lemon juice
2   pounds (25 to 30 count per pound) shrimp, peeled
½   cup flour
2   cups Zatarain's fish fry
1   tablespoon salt
1   tablespoon pepper
    Frying oil

In a bowl, mix eggs, milk and lemon juice. Add shrimp to mixture and let sit for 5 minutes. Remove shrimp from mixture. In another bowl mix flour, fish fry, salt and pepper and dip the shrimp into the mixture. Deep fry until lightly golden brown in oil.

Serves 6 to 8

Kendall "Flounder" Michel

Brett and
Kendall "Flounder" Michel

SHRIMP PO' BOY

3   pounds (50 to 60 count per pound) shrimp, fried - can substitute with oysters or fish
3   tablespoons mayonnaise
1   loaf French bread, pressed if available
1   fresh tomato, sliced
6   pieces fresh lettuce

Fry shrimp according to above recipe. Spread mayonnaise on bread; add shrimp. Cover with tomatoes and lettuce. Fold French bread together and eat as a sandwich.

Serves 4 to 6

Brett Favre

FAVRE FAVORITE FAMILY

GRILLED SHRIMP

2   cups teriyaki sauce
1   tablespoon soy sauce
1   tablespoon oregano
¼   cup parsley
2   tablespoons lemon juice
1   tablespoon salt
1   tablespoon pepper
1   pound (15-20 count per pound) shrimp

In a large bowl, mix together teriyaki sauce, soy sauce, oregano, parsley, lemon juice, salt and pepper. Add shrimp to mixture and marinate (covered) in refrigerator for at least 5 hours. Remove shrimp from marinade and grill for 5-7 minutes on medium heat, turning once.

Serves 2 to 4

Jeff Favre

Young Brett Favre after a long day of fishing.

BROILED SHRIMP

½   stick butter
2   tablespoons garlic powder
2   tablespoons lemon juice
½   teaspoon salt
½   teaspoon pepper
1   pound (15-20 count per pound) shrimp

Melt butter. Add remaining ingredients, except shrimp. Mix well. Butterfly the shrimp and add to the mixture. Marinate for 1 hour. Place shrimp in broiling pan and pour mixture over the shrimp. Broil 5 minutes, turning once.

Serves 2 to 4

Destin Brady

CAJUN POPCORN

Note: Cajun popcorn is also wonderful served on a cold salad.

Flour seasoned with cayenne pepper and seasoning salt to taste
7   ounces crawfish tail meat for each person
    Fine mesh strainer
    Frying oil of your preference heated to 360° F
    Cocktail sauce, recipe to follow
    Lemon wedges

Have seasoned flour in large bowl with strainer in the flour. Add crawfish tail meat and coat; shake and strain out excess flour. Put crawfish in deep fryer; cook 2-3 minutes, until crispy. Drain off oil and serve with lemon and cocktail sauce.

Serves 1

COCKTAIL SAUCE:

2   ounces chile sauce
2   ounces ketchup
1   ounce horseradish
½   ounce fresh lemon juice

Mix chile sauce with ketchup. Add in horseradish and lemon juice.

Serves 4

Chef Channing Boyer
Green Bay, WI

BRETT FAVRE'S
STEAKHOUSE

STUFFED SHRIMP

2	pounds (30-40 count per pound) shrimp
¼	cup lemon juice
½	stick butter, melted
1	cup bread crumbs
½	cup Parmesan cheese, grated
1	small onion, chopped
1	green bell pepper, chopped
2	cloves garlic, minced
½	cup green onions, chopped
½	cup parsley
1	cup lump crabmeat

Peel and butterfly shrimp. Pour lemon juice over shrimp and let sit for 25 minutes. In another bowl, mix butter, bread crumbs, cheese, onion, bell pepper, garlic, green onions and parsley. Fold in crabmeat. Stuff shrimp with mixture. Place shrimp on broiler pan and broil for 5-7 minutes until browned.

Serves 4 to 6

Bonita Favre

Bonita and Jeff enjoying the four F's: family, friends, food and fun.

80

SHRIMP & MIRLITON CASSEROLE

6-8   mirlitons
1   large onion, chopped
1   bunch green onions, chopped
½   green bell pepper, chopped
2   stalks celery, chopped
2   cloves garlic, minced
½   cup butter
1 ½   pounds raw shrimp, chopped
1 ½   cups Progresso garlic and herb bread crumbs

Boil whole unpeeled mirlitons until tender. Let cool and split in half. Remove seed and scoop out mirliton from the shell. Sauté onion, green onions, bell pepper, celery and garlic in butter. Add shrimp. Cook until shrimp are pink. Add mirliton and bread crumbs to desired consistency. Place in buttered casserole dish, top with bread crumbs. Bake at 350° F for 1 hour.

Serves 8 to 10

Sandra Smith

Mirlitons are from the squash family. They are known as a vegetable pear. The mirliton tastes like a mixture between an eggplant and a yellow squash.

FIRE CRACKER SHRIMP

Note: You can make this dish as hot or mild as you wish by adding more or less Tabasco, chile flakes or Cajun spice.

1	ounce olive oil
3	ounces red onion, thinly sliced
3	ounces red, green and yellow bell peppers, thinly sliced
2	ounces mushrooms, sliced
1	Roma tomato, diced
1	ounce green onions, sliced
1	teaspoon garlic, chopped
6	large (10-15 count per pound) peeled and deveined shrimp
1	ounce white wine (we use Chablis)
	Dash of seasoning salt
	Dash of Cajun spice
	Splash of Tabasco sauce
	Chile flakes to taste
4	ounces marinara sauce, bought or home made
½	ounce parsley, chopped
	Pasta of your choice, cooked (we use angel hair)
1	ounce fresh Parmesan cheese, grated

Get sauté pan hot; add olive oil. Add onion, peppers, mushrooms, tomato, green onions, garlic and shrimp and sauté for about 3 minutes. Add white wine, seasoning salt, Cajun spice, Tabasco sauce and chile flakes. Cook 1 more minute to reduce wine. Add marinara sauce and simmer until hot. Pour over hot pasta and garnish with parsley and Parmesan cheese.

Serves 1

Chef Channing Boyer
Green Bay, WI

BRETT FAVRE'S
STEAKHOUSE

DC'S QUICK-N-EASY STUFFED FLOUNDER

With this beautiful and delicious dish, your guests will never know how little time it took to make such a masterpiece!

4	fresh flounder (Gig them from the Gulf or - the easy way - pick them up from the market)
1	package Stove Top Stuffing
1	onion, chopped
1	green bell pepper, chopped
1-2	pounds blue crab meat, picked
4	teaspoons of lemon juice
8	tablespoons of melted butter

Preheat oven to 425° F. Clean the fish and remove the head.

To make a pouch in the fish to hold the stuffing, slit a 4-5 inch opening in the flounder, neck to tail fin. Slide the knife inside the slit and separate the meat from the rib bones. Do this for both sides of the slit. (You should be able to slide your fingers between the meat and bone.) This will make a wide pouch inside the fish to hold the stuffing.

Mix together Stove Top Stuffing according to box directions. Add onion, bell pepper and crab meat to the stuffing. Any other favorite seasonings may be added.

Place fish on a pan. (Line the pan with foil and rub with butter to prevent sticking.) Put the stuffing into the pouch of the fish by lifting the meat and pushing the stuffing into the pouches created between the meat and bone. Pile it high! Drizzle each fish with 2 tablespoons of melted butter and 1 teaspoon of lemon juice.

Place in oven and bake for 30-45 minutes. Serve individually on a large plate. Garnish with parsley, lemon wedges, etc.

Serves 4

Danny & Candi Wasilenko

GIGGING

During certain times of the year on the Gulf coast, we go gigging for flounder. Gigging is wading in about a foot of water and spearing the flounder, which is a very flat fish.

STUFFED FLOUNDER

4   flounder
1   pound crabmeat
2   cans shrimp (6-8 ounces)
1 ½   teaspoons liquid crab boil
3 ½   sticks butter
7   tablespoons water
1 ½   sticks butter
1   medium onion, chopped
3   tablespoons celery, chopped
3   tablespoons green onions, chopped
3   tablespoons bell pepper, chopped
2   tablespoons parsley
1-2   cloves garlic, chopped
2   bay leaves
1   teaspoon dry mustard
1   teaspoon Worcestershire sauce
2   cups bread crumbs
4   lemons, sliced

In skillet, sauté seafood, crab boil, 1 stick of butter and 3 tablespoons water until seafood is heated.

In large saucepan, melt 1 stick butter. Add onion, celery, green onions, bell pepper, parsley, garlic, bay leaves, mustard, Worcestershire sauce and bread crumbs . If too dry, add remaining ½ stick of butter and 4 tablespoons of water. Heat thoroughly.

To prepare flounder without cutting through bone, cut down middle of flounder to tail and cut across tail to form a T. Cut 1-2 inches into side of flounder.

Loosely pack pockets with stuffing. Dot each piece of fish with 2 tablespoons of butter and cover with lemon slices. Bake at 350° F approximately 25 minutes or until fish is opaque and flakes easily.

Serves 4

Sandy Adams

BLACKENED TUNA WITH FRESH FRUIT RELISH

The slightly sweet relish helps cut the spice of seasonings on this dish. It also goes nicely with rice or a rice blend.

For Relish:

2	cups fresh pineapple, peeled, cored and diced
1	cup fresh papaya, peeled, seeded and diced
1	cup fresh strawberries, tops removed and diced
¼	cup each red, yellow, green peppers, finely diced
¼	cup red onion, finely diced
1	tablespoon fresh garlic, minced
½	cup olive oil
¼	cup red wine vinegar

For Fish:

6	each 8-10 ounce thick cut fresh tuna steaks (may substitute swordfish or marlin)
2	cups seasoning (Cajun, blackening or Creole)

For relish toss all items together well in a mixing bowl. Cover and refrigerate at least 1 hour. This can be made 1 day ahead.

For fish heat a heavy cast iron pan or sauté pan to very hot on high heat (no oil is needed). Coat fish with seasoning. The heavier the coating of spices, the spicier the fish will be. Put fish in pan and blacken fish on both sides. Time needs to be adjusted depending on the thickness and type of fish. Tuna is best served medium rare. Make sure not to over cook, or fish will be dry. Serve fish topped with a hearty amount of fruit relish.

Serves 6

Chef Dean McArthur
Milwaukee, WI

BRETT FAVRE'S
STEAKHOUSE

SHRIMP BENTZ

Broccoli florets from 3 stalks
1   medium onion, chopped
4   tablespoons butter
1   can Campbell's cream of mushroom soup
¾   cup milk
½   cup water
1   roll Kraft garlic cheese
5   slices Kraft American cheese
1   quart peeled & deveined (30-40 count per pound) shrimp, drained
    Lawry's seasoned salt
4   tablespoons Italian dressing
1   tablespoon Mrs. Dash seasoning
1   package angel hair pasta

Steam broccoli florets until tender. Sauté onion in butter until tender. Stir in cream of mushroom soup, milk and water. Heat until mixture is well blended. Add in garlic cheese and American cheese. After cheese melts, add in broccoli florets. In a bowl, sprinkle shrimp with seasoned salt, then add Italian dressing and toss. Spray wok with cooking spray. Add shrimp after wok is very hot. Stir with wooden spoon dipping excess liquid from wok. Add Mrs. Dash seasoning. Cook until liquid has evaporated. Add shrimp to sauce. Boil angel hair pasta and drain. (Toss with olive oil or cooking oil to prevent sticking.)

Serve sauce over angel hair pasta.

Serves 6 to 8

Helen & Leonard Bentz

CREOLE SHRIMP STEW

1 pound (40-50 count per pound) boiled shrimp
1 10 ¾-ounce can condensed chicken gumbo soup
1 14 ½-ounce can stewed tomatoes
3 small onions, cubed
2 cloves garlic, minced
1 cup water
¾ cup cooked rice
½ teaspoon dried basil
1 bay leaf
1 teaspoon salt
1 teaspoon red pepper sauce

Combine and heat all ingredients to a boil, reduce heat, cover and simmer for 20-25 minutes or until done. Remove bay leaf. Serve.

Serves 4 to 6

Sandy Adams

SHRIMP JAMBALAYA

1 cup onion, chopped
1 cup celery, chopped
1 cup green bell pepper, chopped
2 cloves garlic, minced
½ stick butter
2 tablespoons flour
1 14 ½-ounce can whole tomatoes
1 can tomato sauce (small)
2 cups uncooked conventional rice
2 pounds (40-50 count per pound) shrimp
1 teaspoon salt
1 teaspoon pepper
2 ½ cups water

Sauté onion, celery, bell pepper and garlic in butter until tender. Add flour and mix well. Add tomatoes and sauce and bring to a boil. Add rice, shrimp, salt, pepper and water. Cook covered on low heat until rice is tender. Add more water if mixture is too dry. Add additional salt and pepper to taste if necessary.

Serves 6 to 8

Jeff Favre

SHRIMP SCAMPI

1   small onion, minced
¼   cup of parsley
1   stick butter
2   tablespoons lemon juice
2   tablespoons garlic, minced
1   pound (36-40 count per pound) shrimp
1   teaspoon salt
1   teaspoon pepper
     Tabasco to taste
     Cooked pasta of your choice

Sauté onion and parsley in butter until onion is tender. Add lemon juice and garlic and stir. Add shrimp, salt, pepper and Tabasco sauce. Sauté until shrimp are pink. Serve with pasta.

Serves 4 to 6

Scott Favre

FRIED OYSTERS

1   quart oysters
2   eggs, beaten
¼   cup milk
1   tablespoon salt
1   tablespoon pepper
     Flour
     Zatarain's fish fry
     Frying Oil

Drain oysters and set aside. Mix eggs, milk, salt and pepper. In a separate bowl, combine fish fry and flour in a 3-to-1 ratio. Roll oysters in flour mixture. Dip in egg mixture, then again in flour mixture. Fry at 375° F until golden brown.

Serves 6 to 8

Kendall Michel

OYSTERS FLORENTINE

2 dozen oysters and liquor, shucked
¼ cup onions, chopped
1 clove garlic, minced
½ stick butter
½ cup cooked spinach, finely chopped
¼ cup heavy cream
1 teaspoon salt
1 teaspoon pepper

Drain oysters and set aside, save ½ of the liquor. If large oysters, chop in half. Sauté onions and garlic in butter until tender. Add oysters, ½ the liquor, spinach, cream, salt and pepper. Cook over low heat for 5 minutes, stirring continuously.

Serves 4 to 6

Scott Favre

Scott and Brett in their early baseball days.

OYSTER ARTICHOKE CASSEROLE

4 artichokes
¾ stick butter
2 tablespoons flour
¼ cup green onions, chopped
3 dozen oysters and liquor
1 teaspoon thyme
1 teaspoon salt
1 teaspoon pepper
1 cup bread crumbs
1 cup Parmesan cheese, grated

Boil artichokes until tender. Mash hearts, scrape leaves and set aside. Make light roux (see page 43) with ¼ stick of butter and 2 tablespoons flour. Sauté green onions, oyster liquor, thyme, salt and pepper and artichokes in roux. Sauté oysters in ¼ stick of butter until edges curl. Add to artichoke mixture and cook for 10 minutes on low heat. Place in casserole dish and top with bread crumbs, ¼ stick of melted butter and Parmesan cheese. Bake at 400° F for 10-15 minutes or until golden brown.

Serves 8 to 10

Scott Favre

89

OYSTER PIE

3 dozen oysters and liquor
½ stick butter
2 tablespoons flour
1 large onion, chopped
1 4-ounce can mushrooms
¼ cup parsley
1 can evaporated milk
1 pie shell and top

Drain oysters and save liquor. Sauté oysters in melted butter until they curl. Take oysters out. Make a roux (see page 43) with flour and butter left in pan. Add onion and mushrooms, and cook until tender. Add oyster liquor, parsley and milk. Stir until thick. Add oysters. Pour in pie shell and cover with pie top. Cook for 20 minutes at 350° F or until golden brown.

Serves 6 to 8

Scott Favre

OYSTERS & PASTA IN CREAM

2 sticks butter
1 cup green onions, chopped
1 clove garlic, minced
3 cups heavy cream
3 dozen oysters and liquor
½ cup fresh parsley
1 ½ pounds cooked pasta
Salt to taste (optional)
Pepper to taste (optional)

Melt 1 stick of butter over medium heat. Add green onions and garlic and cook for 2 minutes. Gradually add in cream, whisking constantly until it thickens. Add remaining butter and stir until sauce thickens. Add oysters, liquor and parsley. Cook until edges of oysters curl. Then add pasta and mix well until pasta is coated with sauce. Add salt and pepper to taste if necessary. Serve immediately.

Serves 6 to 8

Scott Favre

FRIED FISH FILLETS

2 eggs
1 cup milk
   Dash of Tabasco sauce
1 tablespoon lemon juice
4 fish fillets (fresh speckled trout are my favorite)
1 bag Zatarain's fish fry
1 ½ teaspoons salt
1 teaspoon pepper
   Frying oil

Mix eggs, milk, Tabasco sauce and lemon juice, and set aside. Drench fillets in egg mixture. In separate bowl, mix fish fry, salt and pepper. Coat fillets with fish fry and fry until golden brown. This recipe may be used with trout, bass, flounder or catfish.

Serves 4

Scott Favre

TROUT A LA CLARK

2 trout fillets
1 can Rotel tomatoes
1 tablespoon garlic powder
¼ cup parsley
½ stick butter
   Dash of lemon juice
   Salt to taste
   Pepper to taste

Place fish on a large sheet of aluminum foil. Place all ingredients on top of fish and seal foil. Place in oven and bake at 350° F for 15-20 minutes.

Serves 2

Clark Henegan

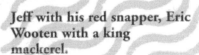

Jeff with his red snapper, Eric Wooten with a king mackerel.

Growing up on the Gulf Coast we ate many types of fish. Whether salt water or fresh, it was always good.

PIROGUE'S GRILLED REDFISH

1   large red fish fillet with scales
     lemon butter sauce (see page 44)

Make vertical and horizontal cuts along fillet of fish. Baste fish with lemon butter sauce and place on grill, scale side down. Continue to baste while cooking. Cook until fish flakes and turns white.

Serves 2 to 4

Glenn Rose

BLACKENED REDFISH

4   8-ounce redfish fillets
3   sticks butter, melted
     Blackened seasoning (Paul Prudhomme's or other)

Heat butter in large cast iron skillet until smoking. Set 2 or 3 tablespoons of butter to the side. Dip each fillet in butter so that both sides are well coated. Sprinkle seasoning generously on both sides. Pat seasoning in by hand. Place fillets in hot skillet and cook approximately 2 minutes at 400° F on each side or until sides are charred. Add in the butter set aside before frying each fish.

Serves 4

Lloyd Nicaud

FRIED TROUT WITH CRABMEAT & CREAM SAUCE

6   fried trout fillets (recipe for fried trout on page 91)
1   onion, chopped
1   green bell pepper, chopped
1   clove garlic, minced
2 ½ sticks butter
1   cup mushrooms, chopped
¼   cup green onions, chopped
1   pound crabmeat
¼   cup parsley

Sauté onion, bell pepper and garlic in butter until tender. Add in mushrooms and green onions and cook on high for 5 minutes. Add crabmeat and parsley and serve with trout. Pasta may also be used. May add crawfish or shrimp to crabmeat or substitute either one.

Serves 4 to 6

Scott Favre

BROILED RED SNAPPER

1   stick butter
2   tablespoons lemon juice
1   tablespoon garlic powder
1   tablespoon Worcestershire sauce
¼   cup parsley
1   teaspoon salt
1   teaspoon pepper
4   red snapper fillets

Melt butter and add all ingredients except fish. Mix well. Place fish on baking or broiling pan and pour butter mixture over fish. Broil uncovered for 12-15 minutes or until browned.

Serves 2 to 4

Irma Mallini

QUICK CREOLE JAMBALAYA

¾	cup onions, chopped
½	cup celery, chopped
½	cup green bell pepper, chopped
1	clove garlic, minced
2	tablespoons parsley
¼	teaspoon pepper
2	tablespoons melted butter
1	28-ounce can tomatoes
1	10 ½-ounce can beef broth
1 ¼	cups water
1	cup uncooked conventional long grain rice,
1 ½	pounds (40-50 count per pound) fresh shrimp, peeled and deveined

Cook onions, celery, bell pepper, garlic, parsley and pepper in butter over medium heat stirring constantly until vegetables are tender. Stir in tomatoes, beef broth and water. Bring to boil, stir in rice, cover, reduce heat and simmer 20 minutes. Add shrimp to rice mixture. Bring to boil, cover and reduce heat. Simmer until shrimp turn pink.

Serves 6 to 8

Aunt Audrey Lyons

MEEMAW'S SUPER BOWL XXXI SHRIMP CREOLE

1   medium onion, chopped
2   bunches green onions, chopped
3   cloves garlic, minced
1   small stalk celery, chopped
1   small green bell pepper, chopped
4   tablespoons cooking oil
2   10 ½-ounce cans Del Monte tomato sauce
2   tablespoons of Mrs. Dash
     Tony Chachere's seasoning to taste
4   pounds (40-50 count per pound) shrimp, peeled
2   cups cooked rice

Sauté onion, green onions, garlic, celery and bell pepper in cooking oil over low heat for 2 minutes. Add tomato sauce, Mrs. Dash and Tony Chachere's seasoning. Simmer on low for 1 hour. Add shrimp to the mixture and simmer for about 30 minutes. Serve over rice.

Serves 8 to 10

Izella (Meemaw) French

FAVRE FAVORITE FAMILY

This was the Favre family's first meal together after Super Bowl XXXI, which Brett jokingly named Meemaw's Super Bowl Shrimp Creole.

SEAFOOD PASTA

⅓   cup onion, chopped
½   pound (40-50 count per pound) shrimp
½   pound crawfish
4   crabs or ½ pound crabmeat
6   tablespoons butter
2   tablespoons water
1 ½ teaspoons liquid crab boil
¼   cup flour
¼   teaspoon dry mustard
½   teaspoon salt
¼   teaspoon pepper
1 ½ cups whole milk
1   cup Velveeta cheese, cubed
1   2 ½-ounce jar sliced mushrooms
1   package angel hair pasta, cooked
3   green onions, chopped

In skillet, sauté onion and seafood in 2 tablespoons butter, 2 tablespoons water and 1 ½ teaspoons (or to taste) liquid crab boil until shrimp are pink. Set aside. Mix flour, mustard, salt and pepper with remaining butter in saucepan. When butter is melted, stir mixture until slightly browned. Gradually add milk to make white sauce. When sauce is thick, add cheese. Stir until cheese melts. When cheese is completely melted, add drained seafood and mushrooms. Allow seafood to heat through. Simmer about 5 minutes. If sauce is too thin, add more cheese. If sauce is too thick, add more milk. Serve over pasta and sprinkle with chopped green onions.

Serves 6 to 8

Sandy Adams

MEEMAW FRENCH'S
SHRIMP & EGGPLANT CASSEROLE

4	medium eggplants, peeled and cut in small chunks
1	tablespoon of salt
1	medium onion, chopped
½	celery stalk, chopped
½	bunch green onions, chopped
3	cloves garlic, chopped
2	tablespoons of olive oil or ½ stick butter
3	pounds (40-50 count per pound) shrimp, peeled
1	stick of butter
1	cup bread crumbs
2	tablespoons Mrs. Dash
1	teaspoon Tony Chachere's to taste

Boil eggplant and salt in enough water to cover, until water is dark. Drain in colander. Sauté onion, celery, green onions and garlic in olive oil or ½ stick butter on low heat about 3 minutes. Add the drained eggplant to the seasonings. In another pan, sauté shrimp in ¼ stick of butter until they turn pink. Add shrimp to eggplant mixture. Add ¾ cup of bread crumbs to mixture. Pour in a buttered pan. Sprinkle top with remaining bread crumbs and ¼ stick melted butter. Sprinkle Mrs. Dash and Tony Chachere's seasoning on. Bake uncovered for 45 minutes at 300° F.

Serves 8 to 10

Izella (Meemaw) French

SHRIMP & EGGPLANT CASSEROLE

3	large eggplants, peeled and cut in bite-size pieces
1	stick butter
1	onion, chopped
1	green bell pepper, chopped
2	stalks celery, chopped
1	tablespoon salt
1	tablespoon pepper
2	pounds (40-50 count per pound) shrimp
½	cup bread crumbs
1 ½	cup shredded mozzarella cheese

Boil eggplant until tender. Drain and sauté eggplant in butter with onion, bell pepper, celery, salt and pepper for 10 minutes. Add shrimp and bread crumbs and cook for 10 more minutes. Pour into casserole dish and bake uncovered for 35 minutes at 350° F. Remove and cover with cheese. Bake for 10 minutes.

Serves 6 to 8

Cindy Doyle Schubert

STUFFED FLOUNDER

1   fresh flounder
     Salt to taste
     Pepper to taste
1   tablespoon lemon juice
¼   cup margarine, melted
1   onion, chopped
1   cup celery, chopped
1-2 cloves garlic, chopped
1   green bell pepper, chopped
1   can white crabmeat
2-3 eggs
4-8 bread slices

Wash flounder thoroughly and pat dry. Open up cavity by slitting the top portion down the backbone and folding each side outward. Salt and pepper to taste. Mix lemon juice and butter. Place the flounder on tin foil that has been spread with some of the lemon/butter mixture. Sauté the onion, celery, garlic and bell pepper until tender. Add the crabmeat, eggs and bread slices to desired consistency (soften bread slices with water or milk) to the vegetable mixture. Mix well and stuff into prepared flounder. Pour additional butter/lemon juice liquid on top of the stuffed flounder and close cavity. Cover with tin foil and bake at 325° F for approximately 45 minutes to 1 hour or longer until done. Do not over cook!!!

Serves 1 to 2

Peggy Ladner

Scott, Jeff and family dog, Whiskey.

Jeff and his big catch.

99

Brett

Jeff

Scott

POULTRY AND EGGS

This food group is probably the most versatile of all. Eggs are used so many ways. Not only are they a breakfast food, but also used in salads, batters, appetizers, desserts and are fillers for many meat dishes.

The use of the egg brings to mind two very distinct traditions within our family; the first was every Friday. Mom always had breakfast on the table when she woke us up each morning. But, on Fridays, we had what she called a Touchdown Breakfast, which was really a buffet of all of our favorites (french toast, bacon, scrambled eggs with green onions); a Favre tradition long before Shoney's! The other tradition: All three of us boys were tall, lanky, skinny kids. We were born big. Mom thought she was going to have all fat kids. But, the taller we got, the thinner we got. Mom would buy protein mix to try to fatten us up. What we didn't know was that she not only added milk and ice cream, but raw eggs. But now, rather than trying to gain weight, we all seem to have to work at keeping the weight off. For that reason, chicken has become a major entree on our dinner table.

We have found so many ways to prepare chicken, simply or as an elegant main dish. It can be boiled, baked, stewed, roasted, grilled, broiled, sautéed, fried and put in salads, gumbos and soups. Turkey works too!

Chicken also brings to mind a good friend. While students at the University of Southern Mississippi (USM), Scott and Brett met a guy named Clark Henegan. They became friends and brought him home one weekend. He quickly became a permanent fixture and another boy with a big appetite in the house. We boys didn't mind, especially when Dad started dishing out chores. Mom even started calling him Clark Favre. His claim to fame in the cooking category is Chicken a la Clark, which he concocted on his night to cook - and he now shares it with the world in this cookbook.

Once, when Brett was about 12 years old, he decided he would fry some eggs. Mom smelled something burning and went into the kitchen. Brett had put Karo syrup in the skillet and was heating it. It began to burn and had smoked up the whole kitchen. Lesson learned - never try to fry anything in Karo syrup!

Jeff Favre

DEEP FRIED TURKEY

You will need an injector for this recipe.

Once you eat a fried turkey, you will never want to eat another baked turkey again.

1 whole dressed turkey, thawed
  Creole seasoning
  Creole marinade (refer to page 44)
3-5 gallons peanut oil

Let turkey thaw in refrigerator for a couple of days. Remove giblets and neck. Coat turkey well with seasoning. Inject turkey with marinade in legs and breast. Deep fry in oil at 375° F. Fry 3 ½ minutes per 1 pound of turkey.

Serves 12 to 15

CHICKEN POT PIE

2   cups mixed vegetables
1   can cream of chicken soup
1   cup cooked chicken, chopped
1   teaspoon salt
1   teaspoon pepper
1   teaspoon basil
1   cup Bisquick
½   cup milk
1   egg

Mix vegetables, soup, chicken, salt, pepper and basil together and pour into a 9" baking dish. Mix Bisquick, milk and egg together and pour over vegetable mixture. Bake at 400° F for 30 minutes.

Serves 6 to 8

Wilda McNatt

Meemaw, Uncle Mitt, Brett and Kay Kay tackling a fried turkey.

GRILLED CHICKEN TERIYAKI

1	cup teriyaki sauce
1	teaspoon basil
1	teaspoon oregano
1	teaspoon rosemary
1	teaspoon salt
1	teaspoon garlic powder
1	teaspoon pepper
1	tablespoon olive oil
6	chicken breasts

Mix teriyaki sauce with basil, oregano, rosemary, salt, garlic powder, pepper and olive oil and pour over chicken breasts. Let marinate for 2 hours. Grill chicken on medium heat for 10 minutes on each side.

Serves 4 to 6

Clark Henegan

CHICKEN A LA KING

1	cup onion, chopped
1	cup celery, chopped
1	cup green bell pepper, chopped
1	stick butter
4	tablespoons flour
2	cups chicken breasts, chopped
1	cup chicken stock
1	cup milk
1	4-ounce can mushrooms
1	teaspoon poultry seasoning
	Salt to taste
	Pepper to taste
	Toast

Sauté onion, celery and bell pepper in butter until tender. Add flour, chicken and stock; stir. Cook for five minutes. Add milk and cook for 20 minutes. Add mushrooms and poultry seasoning and cook another 20 minutes on low. Add salt and pepper to taste if necessary. Serve over toast.

Serves 4 to 6

Scott Favre

STUFFED CORNISH HENS WRAPPED IN BACON

2	Cornish hens
	Salt to taste
	Pepper to taste
2	medium onions, chopped in ¼" cubes
1	medium green bell pepper, chopped in ¼" cubes
1	medium apple, peeled and chopped in ¼" cubes
8	slices bacon
1	lemon, quartered
1	cup water
½	cup sherry, or light wine

Season hens inside and out with salt and pepper. Stuff each hen with onions, bell pepper, apple, 2 slices of bacon and lemon, leaving some stuffing aside. Close the cavity with 2 toothpicks. Wrap each hen with 2 slices of bacon and pin with toothpicks in back. Bake at 525° For 15 minutes to sear. Turn down to 375° and bake for 45 minutes. Sauté unused stuffing ingredients with drippings in skillet. Add water and sherry or wine to make gravy. Baste hens with sherry gravy. Split hens, serve breast up with gravy.

Serves 4

Ken Talley

AUNT MERLE'S CORNISH HENS

2	tablespoons butter
1	tablespoon garlic, minced
4	Cornish hens
	Creole seasoning, enough to cover hens lightly
	Pepper, enough to cover hens lightly
	Reynolds oven bags

Melt butter with garlic and brush on hens. Sprinkle Creole seasoning and pepper lightly on hens. Use Reynolds oven bags and follow directions for baking.

Serves 2 to 4

Merle Norfolk

CHICKEN DIVAN

2   bunches fresh broccoli, chopped
1   stick butter
¼   cup flour
1   can Swansons chicken broth
1 ½ cups milk
2   cups Velveeta cheese
½   teaspoon salt
½   teaspoon pepper
¼   teaspoon garlic, minced
8   boneless chicken breasts, cooked and cut into bite size pieces
1   cup fresh Parmesan cheese, grated

Cook chopped broccoli about 5 minutes. Be sure not to over cook.

Cheese Sauce: Melt butter and slowly add flour, stirring out lumps. Add broth, stirring constantly. Sauce will thicken quickly. Add milk to desired consistency. Add Velveeta cheese, salt, pepper and garlic.

In a buttered casserole dish, layer cooked broccoli, then cheese sauce, then chopped chicken breasts. Top with remaining cheese sauce and then cover with fresh grated Parmesan cheese.

Bake at 350° F for 30-45 minutes or until golden brown.

Serves 6 to 8

Sandra Smith

FRIED CHICKEN

2   large frying chickens
1   cup milk
3   eggs
2   teaspoons Tabasco sauce
4   tablespoons salt
4   tablespoons pepper
2   tablespoons garlic powder
3   cups flour
    Vegetable oil for frying
1   large paper bag

Cut chicken into frying size pieces. Wash thoroughly and set aside in colander to drain. In a mixing bowl, mix milk, eggs, Tabasco, salt, pepper, and garlic powder together. In a bowl, pour marinade over chicken and make sure all pieces are coated. Marinate for at least one hour. Place flour in a paper bag. Take chicken from marinade and drop in bag (a few at a time). Close the bag and shake to thoroughly coat chicken. Drop chicken in hot oil and fry at 350° F for 10-20 minutes or until golden brown. (Drain excess on paper towel.)

Serves 8 to 10

Jeff Favre

CHICKEN CACCIATORE

3   pounds chicken, cut up
½   stick butter
1   large onion, chopped
1   clove garlic, chopped
2   cups tomatoes, chopped
1   cup tomato sauce
½   cup chicken stock
1   tablespoon oregano
2   bay leaves
    Salt to taste
    Pepper to taste
8   ounces cooked spaghetti

Season chicken with salt and pepper and brown in butter. Remove chicken and sauté onion and garlic until tender. Add chicken, tomatoes, tomato sauce, stock, oregano, and bay leaves; simmer for 45 minutes. Add salt and pepper. Serve over spaghetti.

Serves 6 to 8

Pat Ladner

CHICKEN & SPAGHETTI WITH CHEESE

1   hen or 2 fryers
1   stick butter
1   cup onion, chopped
1   cup celery, chopped
1   cup green bell pepper, chopped
1   can mushroom soup
1   2-ounce jar diced pimentos
1   package vermicelli spaghetti
6   ounces Parmesan cheese, grated (optional)

Boil chicken until done. Remove skin and bones (save broth). Cut into bite size pieces. In a skillet, melt butter and sauté onion, celery, and bell pepper until soft. Add mushroom soup and pimentos. Let simmer. Cook spaghetti in chicken broth until soft. Mix all ingredients in large casserole dish and top with grated cheese. Bake at 375° F until cheese is melted and spaghetti is hot.

Serves 8 to 10

Bonita Favre

CHICKEN A LA CLARK

1   onion, chopped
1   green bell pepper, chopped
1   tablespoon garlic, minced
1   tablespoon Worcestershire sauce
1   can Rotel tomatoes
3   cans cream of mushroom soup
¼   cup white cooking wine
6   skinless boneless chicken breasts
    Salt to taste
    Pepper to taste
1   tablespoon parsley
½   cup green onions, chopped

Preheat oven to 350° F. Mix onion, bell pepper, garlic, Worcestershire sauce, Rotel, cream of mushroom soup, and cooking wine in a casserole dish. Add chicken breasts, salt, and pepper to taste. Sprinkle parsley and green onions over the top. Bake for 45 minutes at 350° F.

Serves 4 to 6

Clark Henegan

Clark Henegan

UNCLE DEWAYNE'S DANCING CHICKENS

4   frying hens
4   cans beer
1   onion, chopped
2   ounces garlic
1   green bell pepper, chopped
1   tablespoon Tony Chachere's seasoning
1   teaspoon salt
1   teaspoon pepper
½   teaspoon liquid smoke
2   tablespoons BBQ sauce

Clean and wash chickens inside and out. Sprinkle salt, pepper and Tony's seasoning on the inside and outside of chickens. Drink ½ of the beer or pour it out leaving the remainder in the can. Stuff the beer can with all or any of the seasonings and sauces listed, as you can really put anything you want in the beer to season the chicken. Sit each chicken's cavity on a beer can in a pre-heated grill. Close the cover and cook for about 1 hour. The steam from the beer will go through the chickens, keeping them moist.

Serves 6 to 8

Dewayne Mallini

Uncle Dewayne and his famous dancing chickens!

SCRAMBLED EGGS WITH GREEN ONIONS

6   eggs
¼   cup milk
½   cup green onions, chopped
      Salt to taste
      Pepper to taste
2   tablespoons butter or bacon grease

Mix all ingredients, except butter, well. Melt butter and add eggs in large skillet, over medium heat, constantly stirring until soft and fluffy.

Serves 2 to 4

Irvin Favre

HAM, EGG & CHEESE SANDWICH

1   egg
2   tablespoons vegetable oil
1   slice ham
1   slice American cheese
2   slices bread, toasted

Fry egg over easy in vegetable oil. Remove egg and place on toast. Place ham in skillet and heat for one minute. Place cheese on ham until slightly melted. Place on egg and cover with other piece of toast.

Serves 1

Karen Favre

SCRAMBLED EGG & TOMATO SANDWICH

6   eggs
¼   cup milk
1   tomato, chopped
     Salt to taste
     Pepper to taste
2   tablespoons butter or bacon grease
1   tablespoon mayonnaise
4   slices of toast

Mix eggs, milk, tomato, salt and pepper together. In large skillet, melt butter over medium heat. Add egg mixture and cook constantly, stirring until soft and fluffy. Spread mayonnaise on toast and add eggs. Great breakfast sandwich or late night snack.

Serves 2 to 4

Alvin (Rock) Favre, Jr.

Rock and Jade Favre wait for breakfast.

PAWPAW'S PICKLED EGGS

1   dozen eggs
4   tablespoons liquid crab boil
1   cup vinegar in 8 cups boiling water
1   cup beet juice
1   tablespoon salt to taste

Boil eggs and peel. Put in an airtight container and pour remaining ingredients over the eggs.
Let sit for two days before eating.

Serves 8 to 10

Alvin Favre

Pawpaw

MEATS

When it comes to meats I think of barbecues. Barbecuing is one of our favorite activities in life. The main reason for this is our late grandfather, Pawpaw, Alvin Ernest Favre. Pawpaw was a wonderful man. He was the best grandfather a grandchild could ever ask for. Pawpaw had the gift for barbecuing. Whether it was pork chops, beef ribs, chicken or steaks, it always turned out delicious.

Pawpaw would come over early in the morning with two dozen donuts to hold us over until lunch. While we had donuts and coffee, he would entertain us with stories. I can still remember the stories like it was yesterday. After stories and donuts, he would prepare the grill for the meat. He would let the coals burn down until they almost looked like they didn't have any heat, but he would always add a handful every now and then to keep the fire just right. He would cook the meats very slowly, turning them as few times as possible, adding his special barbecue sauce before every turn. You know, I still do not know his exact recipe to this day, but, I think I am pretty darn close. Come lunch time we would all gather around a wooden picnic table. It was a feast.

When the meal was over, everyone was pretty much done for the day. It was time for more storytelling, for catching a few winks with a quick nap, and, after a while, perhaps thoughts of what we would have for dinner....

Jeff Favre

Labats Barbecue

Mr. Horace Labat is a unique gentleman. The quality of this man is reflected in the quality of the food he serves.

From this renovated former grocery store, he serves up what many describe as the best bar-b-que ribs on the coast.

When he hears of someone who is financially distressed, because of a home fire, loss of a job or whatever worthy cause he can assist with, he and his team of volunteers instantly put the wheels in motion for a fund raiser. They begin cooking early in the morning and serve until the last morsel has been consumed. All of this done simply to help another in a time of need.

LABAT'S RIBS

12-16	quarts water
3	tablespoons salt
3	large onions, chopped
4	bulbs garlic, chopped
1	cup granulated garlic
1	cup granulated onion
1	stalk celery, chopped
2	bags Zatarain's crab boil
3	slabs of pork or beef ribs, trimmed of fat
1	bottle barbecue sauce of your choice

Put water and salt in a large pot. Add remaining ingredients except ribs, and let come to a boil.

Add in ribs. Bring back to a boil and let boil for 15 minutes. Remove from water and place on grill. Baste ribs with barbecue sauce and cook until desired color.

Serves 12 to 16

Horace Labat

STEAKS FOR GRILLING

Steak of your choice (filet and ribeye are Favre family favorites)

BASTING SAUCE:

1   stick butter
1   teaspoon pepper
1   teaspoon Tony Chachere's seasoning
1   teaspoon garlic powder
½   cup Worcestershire sauce
½   teaspoon sugar

Mix all ingredients, except steak, well to make marinade. Pour over steaks to marinade. Refrigerate for at least 3 hours. Preheat gas grill for 15 minutes. When you are ready to cook, coat steaks with marinade and place on the grill 3 inches from heat source. Do not keep turning steaks. Turn one time when you see red juices seeping out. Usually 6-8 minutes per side for medium rare, depending on the size of the meat. You can use this basting sauce also for chicken, ribs, pork chops and other meats.

Yields 1 cup

Brett Favre

Pawpaw Favre at work.

MOM'S PEPPER STEAK

1   round steak, cut in strips
2   tablespoons olive oil
1   large green bell pepper, sliced
2   cloves garlic, diced
2   cans French onion soup
1   cup ketchup
¼   cup parsley
1   package egg noodles, cooked

In a large skillet, brown steak strips in olive oil. Add bell pepper and garlic and cook for 5 minutes. Add soup and ketchup and simmer for 15-20 minutes. Add parsley and serve over egg noodles.

Serves 6 to 8

Bonita Favre

SPAGHETTI & MEAT SAUCE

1   pound ground beef
2   medium onions, chopped
2   green bell peppers, chopped
1   clove garlic, minced
½   stick butter
1   14 ½-ounce can whole tomatoes
2   8-ounce cans tomato sauce
2   6-ounce cans tomato paste
¼   cup parsley
2   tablespoons Worcestershire sauce
1   tablespoon sugar
2   bay leaves
1   teaspoon salt
1   teaspoon pepper
1   can mushrooms, chopped
     Cooked spaghetti

Sauté meat, onions, bell peppers and garlic until meat is browned; drain. Add other ingredients, except for the mushrooms and spaghetti, and let simmer for about 2 hours. Add mushrooms and serve over spaghetti.

Serves 6 to 8

Brandi Favre

Brandi Favre was Miss Mississippi American Teen.

MEAT LOAF

2   pounds ground beef
2   eggs, well beaten
1   medium onion, chopped
¼   cup parsley
½   green bell pepper, chopped
3   slices bacon
1   8-ounce can tomato sauce

In a large mixing bowl, mix all ingredients together, except for the bacon and tomato sauce. When mixed well, form it into a loaf and place it in a 9"x 5" loaf pan. Place the bacon over the meat loaf and cover with tomato sauce. Bake at 350° F for 90 minutes.

Serves 6 to 8

Layne Bourgeois

Before cooking or baking ribs or chicken, boil in water and spices for taste and tenderness. See page 111 for boiling recipe.

OVEN BAKED BARBECUED RIBS

4	pounds ribs, cut in pieces
½	cup flour
1	stick butter
1	onion, chopped
1	green bell pepper, chopped
2	cloves garlic, chopped
2	cups barbecue sauce
2	tablespoons Worcestershire sauce
1	cup beef broth
1	teaspoon chili powder
2	teaspoons salt
2	teaspoons pepper

Coat ribs in flour and brown in butter in a cast iron Dutch oven. Add onion, bell pepper, and garlic and cook for 5 minutes. Add remaining ingredients and cook for 3 hours in oven at 300° F.

Serves 6 to 8

Morgan Kowalski

PANEED PORK CHOPS

6 to 8	pork chops
½	cup flour
1	teaspoon garlic powder
1	tablespoon salt
1	tablespoon pepper
¼	cup olive oil

Coat pork chops with flour, garlic powder, salt and pepper. Heat olive oil in large skillet and cook pork chops about 8 minutes on each side until golden brown.

Serves 4 to 6

Scott Favre

Don't bother Jade while she's eating her pork chops!

STUFFED PORK CHOPS

6   thick center cut pork chops
½   cup flour
2   teaspoons salt
2   teaspoons pepper
3   tablespoons olive oil
    Crawfish dressing (see below)

Coat pork chops with flour, salt and pepper. Heat olive oil in large skillet. Brown pork chops on each side. Remove and cut slits in sides of each pork chop to form a pouch. Stuff pork chop with crawfish dressing (recipe following) and bake in oven at 350° F for 25-30 minutes.

Serves 4 to 6

Scott Favre

The Favre family, Alvin, Mary and kids.

CRAWFISH & CORNBREAD DRESSING

1   cup onion, chopped
1   cup celery, chopped
1   cup green bell pepper, chopped
1   clove garlic, chopped
1   stick butter
1   pound pre-cooked crawfish tails
¼   cup parsley
2   cups bread crumbs
2   cups corn bread stuffing mix
6   cups chicken broth
4   eggs
½   teaspoon salt to taste
1   teaspoon pepper to taste

Sauté onion, celery, bell pepper and garlic in butter until tender. Add crawfish tails and cook for 5 minutes. Remove from heat and let cool. Add remaining ingredients and pour into casserole dish and bake at 375° F for 30 minutes.

Serves 4 to 6

Scott Favre

BRISKET

1   10- or 16-ounce bottle Coke™
1   envelope dry onion soup mix
1   bottle Heinz chili sauce
1   5- to 8-pound brisket, trimmed of fat

Place brisket in Dutch oven and add all ingredients. Bake at 350° F for 30 minutes per pound.

Serves 6 to 8

Joan Lacoste

EASY BUT NOT QUICK ROAST & GRAVY

         Cooking oil
3 to 4   pounds roast (sirloin tip is my favorite!)
½   clove fresh garlic, sliced thinly
½   cup flour
1   packet dry onion soup mix
2   cans beef broth
1   can cream of mushroom soup

Bonita and Pat

In a Dutch oven, pour just enough oil to cover the bottom of the pot. Allow the oil to warm on medium to high heat. While oil is heating, use sharp knife to put slits in roast. Then stuff with garlic. Quantity of garlic depends on one's own taste. Then baste the entire roast with flour. When oil is hot, place roast in oil and allow it to brown on each side. When roast has browned on each side, lower fire to a low/simmer heat. Mix onion soup mix, beef broth and cream of mushroom soup together and pour into pot. Stir all together, cover pot and let cook on low for about 3 to 4 hours. Cooking time may vary depending on size of roast, kind of roast and your individual preference. Stir occasionally to prevent sticking. If you prefer to cook in oven, follow recipe until roast has browned. Place roast along with all natural juices and gravy in a large roasting pan and add other ingredients. Cook on a low heat in oven for about 3 to 4 hours. Season with salt and pepper as needed. If using larger roast (5 to 7 pounds), use 3 cans of beef broth.

Serves 4 to 6

Pat Ladner

LASAGNA

3   pounds ground meat
1   2-pound 13-ounce bottle Ragu sauce - your choice of flavor
½   cup water
12 ounces cottage cheese
1   heaping tablespoon dried parsley
3   pounds mozzarella cheese, shredded
1   10-ounce box lasagna noodles

Grease 9" x 12" casserole pan. Brown meat, drain grease and add sauce to meat. Add water, turn to low heat and simmer for ½ hour. In a bowl, mix cottage cheese, parsley, and 1 ½ pounds of the mozzarella cheese. Layer uncooked noodles, meat sauce, cheese mixture, more noodles, meat sauce, etc., ending with sauce. Sprinkle remaining cheese over sauce. Cover with foil and bake at 350° F for 30 minutes. Remove foil and cook 15 more minutes. Do not get it too dry.

Serves 8 to 10

Penny Tripp
Christy Peterson

MEEMAW FRENCH'S HAMBURGER STEAK

Meemaw would always cook this when asked, and she was asked a lot!

6   pounds ground beef
6   large onions, sliced
2   tablespoons Mrs. Dash
1   teaspoon salt
1   teaspoon pepper
1   tablespoon parsley

Make hamburger patties 3 times the size of regular patties. Brown patties on both sides, medium rare. Drain excess fat from pot, reserve 2 tablespoons of oil. Add onions to oil, cook slowly for 10 minutes. Add Mrs. Dash, salt and pepper to the onions and oil and mix. Then add patties. Add water to just cover the patties. Cook for 15 -20 minutes on low heat. Sprinkle with parsley.

NOTE: 2 tablespoons corn starch to a cup of water will thicken your gravy.

Serves 8 to 10

Izella (Meemaw) French

WILD GAME

Growing up on fifty-two-and-a-half acres in the country and on a bayou provided us with a location to hunt and fish. Only 12 acres were cleared, so we had plenty of woods.

There are lots of stories. However, one sticks out in my mind more vividly than others. While Scott was in high school, he would get up early in the morning and go hunting before school. He mainly hunted squirrel and some rabbit. At this time, we had a St. Bernard named Whiskey, which, if you can believe it, would tree squirrels. It was an amazing sight to see. He would tree a squirrel by barking, then he would jump up on the tree. Whiskey weighed about 140 pounds, so he would almost knock small trees down. The poor squirrels were probably scared to death of him.

One day, while hunting, Scott heard Whiskey howling very loudly. He ran to see what was wrong with him. When Scott found him, he had been caught in a steel trap that had been set to catch raccoons. Seeing that Whiskey was in severe pain, Scott tried to release him, but Whiskey bit Scott on the leg. Scott ran all the way home crying.

Upon arriving home, Dad asked what was wrong, but Scott was so upset he couldn't talk. Dad told him to just tell him. When they got back to Whiskey, he was still in the trap in pain. Dad had to go get the trap-setters and have them get Whiskey out. They had to stick a piece of wood in his mouth, while another one freed the trap from his leg. When he was released, Whiskey ran straight for Dad. Whiskey needed some love, some reassurance.

One fishing story I remember quite well is about Brett. He wasn't the best guy to have around when we had a big catch. One day Scott, Brett, and Dad were fishing in a lake near the house. Scott and Dad did most of the fishing and caught the majority of the fish, while Brett simply played around. Toward the end of the day they had a stringer full of bass. Dad soon noticed that the stringer of fish was swimming past him. He asked Brett if he had tied the stringer. Unfortunately, the answer was no. Needless to say, they lost all of the fish and Brett didn't get invited to go fishing too many times after that.

Jeff Favre

Saturday Morning

The many lakes and bayous of southern Mississippi have much to offer those who prefer hunting or fishing. Imagine a quiet Saturday morning, a buddy, a cooler full of ice, and the anticipation of landing the big one.

It's a tough job, but somebody's gotta do it.

LLOYD'S BACON WRAPPED DOVES

10-12	dove breasts
10-12	bacon slices
	Salt to taste
	Pepper to taste

Wash dove breasts and pat dry. Season each breast with salt and pepper. Wrap each breast with a slice of bacon. Place doves on grill and cook for 45-60 minutes on low heat.

Serves 6 to 8

Lloyd Nicaud

DOVE STEW

12	dove breasts
	Salt to taste
	Pepper to taste
½	cup flour
1	cup oil
1	onion, chopped
1	stalk celery, chopped
1	green bell pepper, chopped
1	carrot, chopped
2	cans beef broth
2	cups rice, steamed

Wash dove breasts and pat dry. Season with salt and pepper and coat with flour. Brown breasts in hot oil in Dutch oven. Remove breasts from oven. Put onion, celery, bell pepper and carrot in Dutch oven and sauté for 5 minutes. Add more flour to pick up any excess oil. Add broth and dove back to mixture and bring to boil. Reduce heat to low and cook for 45 minutes. Serve with rice.

Serves 6 to 8

Scott Favre

You
should try my
Dove Stew!

SCOTT'S STUFFED QUAIL

1   pound (20-25 count per pound) shrimp
1   package bacon
6   quail
    Salt to taste
    Pepper to taste
½   cup flour
1   stick butter
1   cup onion, chopped
1   cup green bell pepper, chopped
2   cloves garlic, chopped
1   cup shrimp stock (refer to page 43)
¼   cup parsley
1   cup cooked rice

Wrap shrimp in bacon and sauté for 5 minutes on medium to high heat and remove from stove. Clean quail and pat dry. Season with salt and pepper lightly and coat with flour. Brown quail in bacon fat and butter in a Dutch oven. Remove from oven. Stuff quail with bacon wrapped shrimp. Add onion, bell pepper and garlic in pan and sauté for 5 minutes. Add remaining shrimp, stock, parsley and quail back to the pot and bring to a boil. Reduce heat. Add rice (salt and pepper if necessary to taste) and cook on low for 30-45 minutes.

Serves 4 to 6

Scott Favre

FRIED QUAIL

1   egg
1   cup milk
6   quail
2   cups flour
2   tablespoons salt
2   tablespoons pepper
1   tablespoon garlic powder
     Oil for frying

Mix egg and milk together. Cover quail with milk and egg mixture. Let sit for 1 hour. Mix flour, salt, pepper and garlic powder. Heat oil to 350° F and cook quail for 10-15 minutes or until golden brown.

Serves 4 to 6

Scott Haas

Scott Haas

GRILLED QUAIL

6   quail
1   cup teriyaki sauce
1   tablespoon lemon juice
1   tablespoon Tabasco sauce
2   tablespoons pepper
1   tablespoon salt
1   tablespoon garlic powder

Clean quail. Mix all ingredients together in a large mixing bowl. Marinate quail in covered container for 24 hours in refrigerator. Grill for 8-12 minutes close to fire.

Serves 4 to 6

Jeff Favre

PANEED DUCK

2   duck breast fillets
1   egg
1   cup half & half
1   tablespoon salt
1   tablespoon pepper
    Bread crumbs
1   stick butter

Pound duck breasts with mallet. Combine egg, half & half, salt and pepper together. Dip duck in egg mixture, then in the bread crumbs. Cook on medium to high heat in butter for 3-5 minutes on each side or desired degree of thoroughness.

Serves 2 to 4

Scott Favre

STOVE TOP DUCK

2   medium sized ducks
2   tablespoons salt
2   tablespoons pepper
1   large onion, chopped
1   green bell pepper, sliced
2   cloves garlic, chopped
1   can cream of mushroom soup
½   cup water
¼   cup parsley
1   stick butter
2   cups cooked rice

Season ducks inside and out with salt and pepper. Stuff each duck with a little onion, bell pepper, garlic; brown duck. Remove from pot. Add the rest of vegetable mixture to the pot and sauté for 5 minutes. Add soup, water and ducks to pot and bring to a boil. Reduce heat to low and cook for 45 minutes covered. Add parsley. Serve with rice.

Serves 2 to 4

Chad Favre

I love rabbit hunting with Stevie. He always has something to eat during or after the hunt. Stevie will cook a big pot of jambalaya, beans or gumbo. He will start early that morning right after daybreak. Before noon everyone gathers around the fire and listens to each other's tall tales. Then we all enjoy Stevie's good cooking.

– Jeff Favre

FRIED RABBIT

1	rabbit, cut up
1	cup milk
1	cup flour
1	teaspoon garlic powder
	Oil for frying
1	teaspoon salt
1	teaspoon pepper

Wash rabbit and pat dry. Marinate rabbit in milk at least one hour. Dredge in flour, garlic powder, salt and pepper. Fry in hot oil until tender, turning frequently.

Serves 2 to 4

Stevie Haas

BARBECUED RABBIT

1	rabbit, cut up
1	onion, chopped
1	green bell pepper, chopped
2	cloves garlic, chopped
2	tablespoons Worcestershire sauce
2	tablespoons lemon juice
2	cups barbecue sauce
1	teaspoon salt
1	teaspoon pepper

Wash rabbit and pat dry. Place in a baking dish. Mix remaining ingredients together and pour over rabbit. Bake for 60 minutes, covered at 325° F. Uncover and bake for another 10 minutes at 375° F.

Serves 2 to 4

Scott Haas

SMOTHERED RABBIT

2   rabbits, cut up
     Salt to taste
     Pepper to taste
1   stick butter
1   large onion, chopped
1   green bell pepper, chopped
2   stalks celery, chopped
2   cloves garlic, chopped
2   tablespoons Worcestershire sauce
2   cans cream of mushroom soup
1   cup water
2   cups cooked rice

Wash rabbits and pat dry. Season rabbits with salt and pepper. In Dutch oven, brown rabbits in butter. Remove rabbits and add in onion, bell pepper, celery and garlic, cooking until tender. Add remaining ingredients except rice, and return rabbits to pot. Cook on low for 1 ½ hours or until rabbits are tender. Serve with rice.

Serves 4 to 6

Stevie Haas

Stevie Haas and Mike Favre get ready to dig in.

FRIED SQUIRREL

2   squirrels, cut up
1   cup milk
1   cup flour
1   teaspoon garlic powder
1   teaspoon salt
1   teaspoon pepper
     Oil for frying

Clean squirrels. Marinate squirrels in milk at least one hour. Mix together flour, garlic powder, salt and pepper. Dredge squirrels in flour mixture. Fry in hot oil until tender, turning frequently.

Serves 2 to 4

Jeff Favre

FRIED DEER TENDERLOIN

1	deer tenderloin
1	cup milk
2	cups flour
1	tablespoon salt
1	tablespoon pepper
1	tablespoon garlic powder
	Oil for frying

Cut tenderloin in small steaks, ½" thick. Pound steaks with mallet to tenderize. Place steaks in milk. In a separate bowl, mix flour and seasonings. Coat each steak well with flour and seasonings. Fry for a few minutes at 350° F on each side until golden brown.

Serves 2 to 4

Chad Favre

GRILLED DEER TENDERLOIN

1	deer tenderloin
2	cups teriyaki sauce
1	tablespoon garlic powder
¼	cup parsley
1	tablespoon salt
1	tablespoon pepper

Cut tenderloin into 1 to 1 ½" thick steaks. Mix other ingredients in a bowl and marinate steaks overnight covered. Grill over low to medium heat until medium rare, basting frequently with remaining marinade.

Serves 2 to 4

Glen Rose

ROASTED VENISON

1   (4-5 pounds) venison roast
2   cloves garlic, sliced
¼   cup vinegar
16 ounces Italian dressing
1   onion, sliced

Cut slits in roast and place pieces of garlic in slits, saving back a few pieces of garlic. Place in roasting pan and pour vinegar, dressing, onion, and remaining garlic over roast. Bake at 325° F for one hour and forty-five minutes. Baste occasionally.

Serves 4 to 6

Scott Favre

ROTTEN BAYOU ALLIGATOR BROILED WITH LEMON BUTTER SAUCE

4   pounds alligator, trimmed of fat and cut in cubes
2   cups of lemon butter sauce (see page 44)

Lay aluminum foil over barbecue pit or use broiler pan. Adjust heat to low-medium. Baste alligator with lemon butter sauce while on foil or pan. Cook for 5 minutes; baste again. Cook for 10 more minutes, then baste again. Serve immediately

Serves 8 to 10

Jeff Favre

Yes, that's a gator …

ALLIGATOR SAUCE PIQUANT

2 cups white flour
1 cup butter
5 cups white onions, finely chopped
1 cup green onions, chopped
2 cups green bell peppers, finely chopped
1 cup celery, finely chopped
2 cups fresh tomatoes, chopped
1 tablespoon sugar
1 tablespoon Worcestershire sauce
1 tablespoon lemon juice
3 cups tomato sauce
3 cups V-8 juice
1 cup white wine
  Dash Tabasco or hot sauce
3 tablespoons fresh garlic, finely chopped
3 pounds alligator meat, trimmed of fat and cut in cubes
  Salt to taste
  Pepper to taste

Make a roux (refer to page 43) with butter and flour. When roux reaches desired color add onions, green onions, bell peppers, and celery; cover and cook until onions are tender, stirring. Stir in tomatoes and sugar and cook for 10 minutes. Stir in Worcestershire, lemon juice, tomato sauce, V-8, wine, hot sauce and garlic; mix well. Add alligator and enough water to cover the ingredients by a couple of inches; stir. Bring to a boil, stirring frequently. After it cooks 5 minutes, reduce heat to low and cook for 3 hours or until meat is tender. Serve over rice or pasta.

Serves 14 to 16

Chad Favre

Irvin and Bonita at their wedding reception on November 27, 1965.

Irvin and Bonita
celebrating Mardi Gras
at the Long Beach
Carnival Ball in Long
Beach, MS, in 1996.

After a wonderful meal at the Palace Cafe in New Orleans. Scott, Jeff and Brett Favre along with proprietor, Dick Brennan.

Boy, do we hate Mom for submitting this picture from the late '70s.

Jeff and Brandi just told Santa what they wanted for Christmas. They wore him out.

Even Duke, the black lab, helps celebrate and cheer on game days.

Big Irv, Scott, Mom (Bonita), Jeff, Brett and Brandi at Brett's golf tournament.

We all had a great time at Meemaw's surprise 80th birthday party.

Oh, what a day! Brett celebrates victory at Super Bowl XXXI in New Orleans, showing off the Vince Lombardi trophy to the crowd.

The serenity of Rotten Bayou with the Green Bay flag flying on the Favre deck.

Brett and Mom jubilant for the success of his celebrity auction at Casino Magic, Bay St. Louis, MS, May 1999.

Deanna, Brett and Brittany celebrating the wedding of Jeff and Rhonda.

WOW! Getting an engagement ring. Scott and Morgan, Christmas, 1998.

Ten-month-old Jade is not so sure she likes posing for pictures with Mom, Rhonda.

Mom watches Jeff grill his dancing chickens at cousin Jace's high school graduation party.

There is usually something cooking - on this day its crawfish etouffee. Ummm good!

Mouth-watering boiled crawfish, corn and potatoes ready for the gang.

Ahh – a shrimp boil – a usual summer sight around the Favre household. Get the crackers and the cocktail sauce ready!

VEGETABLES

Living in the country over the years has been a great asset to our family in many ways. One of those is being fortunate enough to have the land to plant and grow our own vegetables and fruit. Each year on Good Friday, the seeds and plants are sown with great anticipation for the abundance of the fresh vegetables that would be produced. The crop consists of tomatoes, bell peppers, jalapeno peppers, squash, okra and corn. In addition we have cantaloupe, watermelons, cucumbers, green beans, speckled lima beans and potatoes. There is nothing better than to pick tomatoes and cucumbers and add salt, pepper and Italian dressing. Although the labor of picking, cleaning, canning, making pepper jelly and freezing the vegetables is quite time consuming, the results are well worth the effort. When the children were small, we also had the challenge of keeping them from picking the tomatoes (or any ball-shaped vegetable) and throwing them.

Bonita Favre

When I married into the Favre clan I learned a lot of new recipes; corn stew, lima bean soup with noodles, shrimp spaghetti - dishes with enough calories to run an Olympic track team for a week (or a Favre for a couple of days). In turn, I tried to introduce my new husband, Uncle Jimbo, to some of my family's favorites - turnip greens, collards, vegetables - dishes with fewer calories.

Jimbo tried to get used to my menus. Once he applied for a job that required him to lose weight and for a while he seemed to really appreciate my cooking. Within three months he had lost 20 pounds – his target. However, he had also applied to Mississippi Power Company for work and that did not require weight loss. On the same day he hit his weight goal, he got a telephone call.

The Pigeon Palace

These old barns and equipment sheds are often visible from the many roads in northern Hancock or Harrison counties in southern Mississippi. If you know the owners and can access their property, you can find some real jewels well worth exploring. I'm sure this one is full of creepy crawlies and things that go bump in the night. So take along an old ax handle just in case you rouse one of its residents.

When he hung up the phone he said to me, "I am going to work for the power company. Cook me some biscuits and gravy."

He refused to eat "grass" (anything green) for a long time after that. Eventually, he relented and now enjoys all kinds of vegetables. His favorite, however, is still boiled corn with lots of butter.

Fannie Favre

Neal, Fannie and
Uncle Jimbo

GREEN BEAN CASSEROLE

3   cans French style green beans
2   cans cream of mushroom soup
2   tablespoons soy sauce
2   cans french fried onions
1   cup American cheese, shredded
1   teaspoon salt
1   teaspoon pepper

Heat green beans and drain well. Combine with soup, soy sauce, salt and pepper; mix well. Add half portion of onions and cheese and mix well. Pour into baking dish and cover with remaining onions and cheese. Bake at 350° F for 25 minutes.

Serves 6 to 8

SMOTHERED CABBAGE

1   tablespoon olive oil
⅓   stick butter
2   white onions, chopped
1   tablespoon garlic, chopped
½   cup water
1   tablespoon salt
1   teaspoon pepper
1   teaspoon sugar
1   head cabbage, cut up
1   pound salt pork

Melt oil and butter. Add onions, garlic, and water. Bring to a boil. Add in salt, pepper, and sugar; mix well. Add cabbage and salt pork reducing heat to medium, and cook for 1 hour or until cabbage is tender.

Serves 4 to 6

Nora "NoNo" Spikes

As long as I can remember, I have eaten fresh garden vegetables throughout the year. I'm not much of a gardener, but Uncle Mitt and Dad are always growing gardens. My favorite vegetable is collard or mustard greens. If I can't find them around the house then I look elsewhere. I usually can find them at several fruit and vegetable stands on the side of the road. If that doesn't work, then Coach Ladner always has a beautiful garden. Coach Roland Ladner is the cousin of Larry Ladner, and Hall of Fame basketball coach from our high school, Hancock North Central. He is always welcoming me or Big Irv to his crop. Trust me, greens are always some fine eating. Try our Good Ole Southern Mustard Greens and you will see.

Jeff Favre

GOOD OLE SOUTHERN MUSTARD GREENS

2 bunches mustard or collard greens
½ stick butter
1 large white onion, chopped
1 small yellow onion, chopped
1 tablespoon garlic, chopped
1 package Lipton Onion Soup Mix
   1 cup water
   1 pound salt pork, or pork of your choice
   1 bunch green onions, chopped
   2 tablespoons sugar
   1 teaspoon salt
   1 teaspoon pepper

Soak greens in warm salted water for 15 minutes. Then clean each leaf very well. Cut out heavy stems.

Mix all ingredients except greens and let cook for 20 minutes. Then add greens. Let cook on low to medium heat for 1 hour, or until greens are tender.

Serves 6 to 8

Jeff Favre

Brittany, Jade, "Mama Bo," and Dylan

FRIED OKRA

2 cups fresh okra, washed drained, trimmed of tops and tails and sliced in ½ inch pieces
1 cup corn meal
½ teaspoon salt
¼ teaspoon pepper
   Vegetable oil

Toss okra in mixture of corn meal, salt, and pepper. Fry in hot oil until crispy and golden brown. Drain grease on paper towel.

Serves 2 to 4

Bonita Favre

SMOTHERED OKRA

1   onion, chopped
1   green bell pepper, chopped
1   stick butter
2   quarts fresh okra, chopped
1   can Rotel tomatoes
½   teaspoon salt
½   teaspoon pepper

Sauté onion and bell pepper in butter for 5 minutes. Add okra, Rotel, salt and pepper to bell pepper and onion. Cook on low, covered for 45 minutes to 1 hour.

Serves 6 to 8

Bonita Favre

SHRIMP & CRABMEAT POTATOES

Stuff this in a baked potato shell and bake until heated through for an excellent side dish.

6-8   large white potatoes, peeled and sliced
1   onion, chopped
1   green bell pepper, chopped
1   clove garlic, chopped
1   stick butter
2   pounds (25-30 count per pound) shrimp, peeled
1   cup mozzarella cheese, shredded
1   can evaporated milk
¼   cup parsley
1   pound lump crabmeat

Boil potatoes until tender. Mash coarsely and set aside. Sauté onion, bell pepper, and garlic in butter until tender. Add shrimp and cook another 2 minutes. Add ¾ cup of cheese, milk, parsley, crabmeat and potatoes to onion mixture. Mix together well. Pour into casserole dish and sprinkle with remaining cheese. Bake uncovered for 30 minutes.

Serves 6 to 8

Jeff Favre

SMOTHERED YELLOW SQUASH

1   onion, chopped
1   green bell pepper, chopped
1   stick butter
6-8   yellow squash, peeled and sliced
1   tablespoon garlic powder
1   tablespoon oregano
1   teaspoon salt
1   teaspoon pepper

Sauté onion and bell pepper in butter until tender. Add remaining ingredients and cook for 30-45 minutes, covered on low heat.

Serves 6 to 8

Bonita Favre

CREOLE BUTTER BEANS

     Water
1   pound dried large lima beans
½   stick butter
1   large white onion, finely chopped
1   tablespoon fresh garlic, minced
1   fresh tomato, chopped
1   tablespoon sugar
1   can Rotel tomatoes
1   pound sausage of choice, sliced
     Salt to taste
     Pepper to taste
2   cups cooked rice

Soak beans in enough water to cover, overnight; drain and rinse. Melt butter, add onion and garlic; sauté for 10 minutes. Add in fresh tomato and sugar; sauté for 5 minutes. Add Rotel, beans, sausage and enough water to cover beans by 1 inch. Cook 2 hours or until tender. Add salt and pepper. Serve over rice.

Serves 4 to 6

Jeff Favre

RED BEANS & RICE

	Water
1	pound dried kidney beans
1	onion, chopped
1	clove garlic, chopped
½	stick butter
1	tablespoon flour
1	pound smothered sausage, sliced
1	teaspoon salt
1	teaspoon pepper
2	cups rice, cooked

Soak beans in enough water to cover, overnight; drain and rinse. Sauté onion and garlic in butter until tender. Sprinkle flour in with onion and garlic and mix well. Add sausage and beans with enough water to cover beans. Season with salt and pepper. Cook slowly on low heat for 1 hour or until beans are tender. Serve over rice.

Serves 6 to 8

Brett Favre

SPECKLED BUTTER BEANS

	Water
1	pound dried speckled butter beans
½	onion, finely chopped
5	ounces fresh garlic, finely chopped
1	stick butter
½	pound salt pork
	Salt to taste
	Pepper to taste
2	cups cooked rice

Soak beans in enough water to cover by ½ to 1 inch, overnight; drain and rinse. Sauté onion and garlic in butter for 5 minutes. Add beans and salt pork. Add enough water to cover beans plus 1 inch. Cook for 2 hours or until beans are tender. Be sure not to burn. Add salt and pepper. Serve over rice.

Serves 4 to 6

Jeff Favre

NANNIE'S SWEET POTATO CASSEROLE

All measurements are approximate depending on sweetness of potatoes and what your sweet tooth dictates.

7	large sweet potatoes, peeled then boiled until tender
1	tablespoon all-purpose flour
¾	cup sugar
¼	tablespoon baking powder
1	stick margarine
	Salt to taste
1-2	eggs
1	tablespoon vanilla
1	cup milk
1	jigger whiskey (optional - gives nutty flavor)
1	16-ounce bag of large marshmallows

Mix sweet potatoes in electric mixer. Add in flour, sugar, baking powder, margarine, and salt; mix. Then add eggs, vanilla, milk and whiskey. Mix to about thickness of a cake batter.

Put in a large casserole dish.

Bake at 350° F about 30 minutes until casserole looks a little firm. Remove from oven and cover top with 1 bag of large marshmallows. Return to oven, put on broil, and watch carefully until marshmallows are brown. (It doesn't take long!)

Let sit 5 minutes, then serve.

Serves 8 to 10

Linda French Wittmann

TOMATO JUICE

To retain the natural flavor and color of the tomatoes in the canned juice, pare with stainless steel knives. Do not use copper, brass or iron utensils.

Use only fully ripe, firm tomatoes, preferably of bright color. Wash tomatoes and remove cores. Cut into pieces. Simmer until softened. Do not boil. Immediately put the softened hot tomatoes through a fine sieve. Heat the juice to simmering. Pour into containers to within ¼" of top. Add 1 teaspoon of salt to each quart. Seal. Process in water bath container. (Pint and quart jars 10 minutes.)

Serves 2 to 4

Aunt Audrey Lyons

GAMEDAY TRADITIONS

My favorite time of the year is fall. I love it when the leaves start to turn red, yellow, and orange. The air becomes cool and crisp. The bugs begin to disappear and most importantly, FOOTBALL season kicks off.

I can remember my football years well. That was the most fun I had while growing up. Even though it was fun, it taught me so much about life and living. Football is another occasion that has always brought my family and friends together for good food and fun. In this chapter, you will experience some of our traditional recipes on gameday. I hope you will enjoy them as much as we do.

Jeff Favre

DEVILED EGGS

1   dozen eggs
1   cup mayonnaise
2   teaspoons dry mustard
2   tablespoons sweet pickle relish
1   teaspoon salt
1   teaspoon pepper
      Paprika to taste

Boil eggs and peel. Cut eggs in half (long ways) and separate the yolk from the white. In a mixing bowl, mash the egg yolks with a fork and add all other ingredients except paprika. Mix well and fill each half of the egg with the mixture. After the egg halves are filled, lightly dust with paprika.

Serves 6 to 8

Bonita Favre

PARTY MEATBALLS

This is an easy and great dish for parties, especially for Packer games.

1   pound ground beef
½   cup seasoned breadcrumbs
½   small onion, chopped
½   cup green bell pepper, chopped
½   cup celery, chopped
1   clove garlic, minced
1   egg
1   teaspoon salt
½   teaspoon pepper
½   teaspoon Worcestershire sauce
1   bottle Kraft hot barbecue sauce
1   jar Strawberry preserves

Mix ground beef, breadcrumbs, onion, bell pepper, celery, garlic, egg, salt, pepper, and Worcestershire sauce. Shape into small balls. Bake in 350° F oven for 10-12 minutes. Heat barbecue sauce and preserves in equal amounts (enough to cover meatballs when added) until melted. Add meatballs. Simmer for 30 minutes. Serve in a chafing dish with toothpicks.

Serves 6 to 8

Bonita Favre

MOCK OYSTER DIP

1   small onion, chopped
1   stick butter
2   rolls garlic cheese
2   10-ounce packages frozen broccoli, cooked
1   can stems and pieces mushrooms
1   can cream of mushroom soup
   Worcestershire sauce to taste
   Tabasco sauce to taste

Cook onion in butter until tender; add cheese. Cook over low heat (or microwave) until melted. Add other ingredients. Cook until heated through. Serve with crackers or chips.

Serves 6 to 8

Bonita Favre

CHICKEN & SAUSAGE GUMBO

To make a thicker gumbo, add more roux.

4   cups oil
8   cups white flour
6   pounds onions, coarsely chopped
10 ounces garlic, chopped
6   bunches green onions, chopped
7   gallons water
30 pounds boneless chicken thighs, cut in chunks
6   pounds smoked sausage
5   pounds chicken gizzards (optional)
½   cup filé
   Salt to taste
   Pepper to taste
   Tony Chachere's to taste

Cook roux (refer to page 43) with oil and flour. Add onions, garlic and green onions to water and boil for 15 minutes. Reduce heat. Add roux to water slowly, making sure it does not burn. After all the roux is dissolved, add chicken, sausage, and gizzards. Simmer, uncovered for 1 hour on medium heat. Reduce to low heat, add filé, salt, pepper, and Tony Chachere's seasoning; stir well and cook for an additional 10 minutes. Serve over rice and/or potato salad.

Serves 120 to 150 (or a small parking lot)

Broke Spoke - Kiln, MS

All the Favre's love #4, including Dylan.

FAVRE FAVORITE FAMILY

CHICKEN, CRAB & CORN CHOWDER

2	pounds margarine
2	gallons onions, diced
4	quarts green bell peppers, diced
2	quarts celery, diced
4	gallons water
13	ounces chicken base
15	pounds frozen corn
15	pounds chicken or turkey, cooked and diced
1 ¼	cup Cajun seasoning
½	cup cayenne pepper
1	cup seasoning salt
2	quarts heavy cream
4	12-ounce cans evaporated milk
⅛	teaspoon white pepper
4 ¼	pounds pre-cooked crabmeat

Melt margarine and add 1 ½ gallons of onions. Cook until caramelized. Add in green peppers, celery, and remaining onions to caramelized onions; sauté lightly. Add in water, base, corn, and poultry to sauteed vegetables; simmer. Add in Cajun seasoning, cayenne pepper, and seasoning salt; continue to simmer. In a separate pot, scald the cream. After scalded, add the cream, evaporated milk, and white pepper to the rest of the chowder, stirring well. Let simmer for at least 10 minutes. This is to be divided into 7 quart batches. Just before serving, stir in ½ pound of crabmeat.

Yields 5 gallons

Gerard Tabuis

PARTY POTATO SALAD

40   pounds potatoes
15   dozen eggs
½   gallon mayonnaise
1   quart mustard
48   ounces dill pickles, chopped
Salt to taste
Pepper to taste
Tony Chachere's seasoning to taste

Boil eggs for ten minutes (can add salt to eggs so they peel easier). Boil potatoes until they are done. Peel eggs and potatoes and mix them together. Add mayonnaise, mustard, salt, pepper, Tony Chachere's seasoning, and pickles, mixing well. Serve.

Serves 120 to 150

Broke Spoke - Kiln, MS

Big Irv gets a pie in the face, the price of victory.

SHRIMP & SAUSAGE JAMBALAYA

10	pounds (40-50 count per pound) shrimp
1	tablespoon crab boil
1	stick butter
	Water
3	pounds smoked sausage
4	pounds onions, chopped
2	bunches green onions, chopped
5	ounces garlic, minced
1	green bell pepper, chopped
1	can Rotel tomatoes
1	8 ounce can tomato sauce
1	tablespoon salt
½	tablespoon pepper
3	teaspoons Tony Cachere's seasoning
2	tomatoes, diced
4	pounds rice

Boil shrimp in crab boil, ¾ stick butter, and enough water to cover shrimp, for 3 minutes. Strain shrimp and keep water as stock. Sauté onions, green onions, garlic, and bell pepper in ¼ stick of butter until tender. Add sausage, stock, Rotel tomatoes, tomato sauce, salt, pepper, Tony Chachere's seasoning, and tomatoes and bring to a boil. Add in rice, cover pot and cook on low heat until rice is done. Turn off heat and let stand covered for 30 minutes.

Note: Add more rice per desired consistency.

Serves 20 to 30

Jeff Favre

SOUTHERN STYLE CHILI

Brandi lettered
in basketball one year at the
University of South Alabama.

Water
2 pounds red kidney beans
4 cups onions, finely chopped
1 ¼ pounds garlic, finely chopped
1 ½ sticks butter
2 tablespoons flour
2 tablespoons salt
1 tablespoon pepper
15 pounds ground beef
4 pounds green bell peppers, finely chopped
1 pound red bell pepper, finely chopped
1 gallon tomato sauce
48 ounces Rotel tomatoes
10 tomatoes, diced
48 ounces Spicy V-8
½ tablespoon Tony Chachere's seasoning
½ cup chili powder

Soak beans in enough water to cover, overnight. Drain and rinse. Sauté 2 cups of onions and ¼ pound of garlic in ½ stick butter until tender. Sprinkle flour in with onions and garlic and mix well. Add beans and enough water to cover beans. Season with 1 tablespoon salt and ½ tablespoon pepper. Cook slowly on low heat for 1 hour or until beans are tender.
In another pot, brown ground beef with remaining onions; drain. Add in remaining garlic, butter, green peppers, red peppers, tomato sauce, Rotel tomatoes, diced tomatoes, Spicy V-8, and Tony Chachere's seasoning. Cook for 1 hour. Add the beans and cook for 30 minutes. Add in chili powder, remaining salt, and pepper. Serve with crackers, chopped onions, and grated cheddar cheese.

Serves 20 to 30

Jeff Favre

CREOLE SEAFOOD GUMBO

4	cups oil
8	cups flour
3	pounds large yellow onions, finely chopped
1 ½	pounds white onions, finely chopped
2	pounds tomatoes, diced
5	ounces garlic, chopped
1	celery stalk, finely chopped
2 ½	pounds okra, sliced
1 ½	pounds green bell pepper, finely chopped
1	pound red bell pepper, finely chopped
¾	stick butter
1	tablespoon sugar
8	ounces beef bouillon
64	ounces V-8
14 ½	ounces Rotel tomatoes
30	ounces chicken broth
1	gallon crawfish stock
2	gallons water
½	cup parsley
1	bunch green onions
	Salt to taste
	Pepper to taste
	Tony Chachere's seasoning to taste
1	tablespoon filé (optional)
64	ounces crab claw meat
2	dozen gumbo (blue) crabs, clean and peeled
3	pounds pre-cooked crawfish tails
3	pounds (55-60 count per pound) shrimp
10	cups cooked rice

Make roux (refer to page 43) with oil and flour. Sauté onions, tomatoes, garlic, celery, okra, and peppers in butter and sugar. Add to roux. Cook slowly for 2 minutes. Combine beef bouillon, V-8, Rotel, chicken broth, stock, and water. Bring to a boil, reduce heat, and add to roux. Add in seasonings and simmer for 1 hour. Then add seafood. Cook on low heat for 45 minutes. Serve over rice or with potato salad.

Makes 3.5 gallons

Broke Spoke - Muskego, WI

BREAD & DESSERTS

Sea Oats

In recent years beach maintenance crews with special equipment have created sand dunes on our coast beaches.

Sea Oats and other grasses have been added establishing a root system to strengthen the dune in an effort to prevent sand erosion.

The beach scape has therefore changed. Most say for the better.

If you want the attention of a Favre just say, "Dessert." No need to raise your voice. Some may respond with vague references to a diet and will accept "just a taste" - of each of the fifteen desserts on the table. Others may seem unresponsive but if you are not watching carefully you will see a quick jerk of the head or eyes. That's the indication of a Favre who is either supposed to be dieting or one who has already been into the desserts. The former will glance around furtively before easing past the dessert table and on to a scheduled spot. The face of the latter will sport a satisfied smile as he waits graciously for everyone to be served before deciding he will try just a bite of Uncle Milton's banana polis.

All the Favres I know are good cooks, but most specialize in desserts. I especially miss Mawmaw's coconut cakes.

Fannie Favre

Fannie Favre and John Drana

UNCLE MITT'S CORNBREAD CASSEROLE

½ pound ground beef
¼ cup onion, chopped
½ cup green bell pepper, chopped
1 8 ¾-ounce can whole kernel corn, drained
½ cup tomato soup
½ teaspoon salt
   Dash of pepper
¼ cup flour
¼ cup cornmeal
¾ teaspoon baking powder
¾ teaspoon sugar
   Dash of salt
1 egg, slightly beaten
½ cup milk
1 tablespoon vegetable oil

Cook ground beef, onion and bell pepper until meat is browned and vegetables are tender. Stir to crumble meat. Discard pan drippings. Add corn, soup, salt, and pepper; stir until combined. Spoon mixture into a lightly greased 1 quart casserole dish; then set aside.

Combine flour, cornmeal, baking powder, sugar and a dash of salt. Add in egg, milk and oil, stir until moistened, mixture will thin. Pour over casserole and bake at 375° F for 30-40 minutes or until brown.

Serves 6 to 8

Milton Favre

FAVRE FAVORITE FAMILY

Uncle Mitt and Peggy celebrate.

ARTICHOKE BREAD

¼	cup butter or margarine
2-3	cloves garlic, pressed
2	teaspoons sesame seeds
1	14-ounce can artichoke hearts, drained and chopped
1	cup (4 ounces) shredded Monterey Jack cheese
1	cup Parmesan cheese, grated
½	cup sour cream
1	16-ounce loaf unsliced French bread
½	cup (2 ounces) Cheddar cheese, shredded

Melt butter in large skillet over medium to high heat. Add garlic and sesame seeds; cook, stirring constantly, until lightly browned. Remove from heat. Stir in artichoke hearts and next three ingredients. Cover mixture and refrigerate - let stand 10 minutes before assembling.

Cut bread in half lengthwise. Scoop out center of each half leaving a 1-inch shell; set shells aside. Crumble removed pieces of bread and stir into artichoke mixture. Spoon evenly into shells and sprinkle with Cheddar cheese. Place each half on baking sheet, cover with aluminum foil. Bake at 350° F for 25 minutes, uncover and bake 5 minutes until cheese melts. Cut into slices.

Serves 8 to 10

Pat Ladner

AUNT AUDREY'S MEXICAN CORN BREAD

½   cup corn meal
2   eggs
2   jalapeno peppers, chopped
½   cup green onions, chopped
½   cup green bell pepper, chopped
1   cup sour cream
1   cup white cream corn
½   cup oil
1   cup Cheddar cheese, grated

Mix all ingredients except cheese. Pour ½ mixture into baking dish or iron skillet. Spread ½ cup of grated cheese on top. Pour other half of mixture in pan and top with remaining portion of cheese. Bake at 350° F for 45 minutes.

Serves 6 to 8

Audrey Lyons

GOLETTE

4   cups Bisquick
1 ⅓ cup milk

Mix ingredients together well. Form 2 balls: put on a floured surface and press flat with floured hands. Make cakes the size of large pancakes. Cook on a black iron skillet or griddle sprayed with Pam.

Serves 4 to 6

Bonita Favre

FAVRE FAVORITE FAMILY

CRAWFISH BREAD

1   large white onion, chopped
3   bunches green onions, chopped
3   pounds pre-cooked crawfish tails
1   16-ounce box Pillsbury hot roll mix
1   pound block Cheddar cheese, grated
    Cayenne pepper
    Black olives (optional)
    Jalapeno peppers, chopped (optional)

Sauté onion and green onions until clear, add crawfish tails and cook on medium heat for about 10 minutes. Follow directions on box of hot roll mix for preparing dough. One box of hot roll mix will make 3 large loaves of bread. After letting dough stand for 5 minutes, break dough into 3 even pieces. Roll dough out equally, approximately 18 inches in width, about the size of a large pizza. Spread crawfish and onions evenly over dough to all edges. Sprinkle ⅓ Cheddar cheese and cayenne on top of each loaf. Do the same with the olives and jalapeno peppers if you choose. Roll dough up in a jelly roll fashion and place on cookie sheet, seam down. Bake at 350° F for 25 minutes or until golden brown. Remove from oven and cool 5 minutes. Slice as desired. After being cooked, bread may be frozen for up to 2 weeks. Just thaw a little and heat .

This recipe is actually one given to me by my dear friend, Wilda McNatt, whom I taught with for many years. She also taught all four of our children American history. Her recipe was called Italian Sausage Bread. Instead of crawfish, use 2 pounds of bulk hot sausage. Cube the sausage and cook in the oven at 350° F until done.

Serves 6 to 8

Bonita Favre

Bonita Favre was Queen of the St. Paul Carnival Association Pass Christian Mardi Gras in 1996.

AUNT FANNIE'S RAISIN, ALMOND, OAT LOAF

If you want to make this a "healthy" recipe, use unbleached flour, Rumford baking powder (contains no aluminum), canola oil and low-fat milk. If, at the time, you decide to try this recipe eggs have been banned, use egg substitute, what Jimbo calls "almost eggs."

2	cups quick oats (3 minute, not instant)
1	cup plain flour
1	teaspoon salt
2	teaspoons baking powder
1	teaspoon cinnamon
¼	cup sliced almonds
½	cup raisins
½	cup brown sugar
½	cup oil
1	cup milk
2	eggs
1	teaspoon vanilla
¼	teaspoon butter flavor

Mix dry ingredients and wet ingredients separately. Combine wet and dry ingredients and pour into a greased loaf pan. Bake at 325° F to 350° F for about 1 hour.

If you want to please Uncle Jimbo, use ½ cup melted butter instead of oil, butter the bread when it comes out of the oven, and serve with at least a pint of milk.

Serves 4 to 6

Fannie Favre

UNCLE JIMBO'S LEMON ICEBOX PIE

1   12-ounce box vanilla wafers
4   14-ounce cans sweetened condensed milk
1 ⅓   cup lemon juice
        Cherry, blueberry and strawberry pie filling (optional)

Crumble or grate enough vanilla wafers to cover the bottom of a serving dish. Line the sides of the dish with whole vanilla wafers. Combine the condensed milk and lemon juice until the mixture is very thick. Pour into the vanilla wafer crust and chill well. Serve as is or top with cherry, blueberry or strawberry pie filling.

If more than four Favres are to be served, it is a good idea to make two pies.

Serves 6 to 8

Jimbo Favre

AUNT AUDREY'S OATMEAL COOKIES

This is believed to be the best oatmeal cookie the Favre's have eaten.

1   cup margarine or butter, softened
1   cup brown sugar, firmly packed
½   cup granulated sugar
2   eggs
1   teaspoon vanilla extract
1 ½   cups all-purpose flour
1   teaspoon baking soda
1   teaspoon cinnamon
½   teaspoon salt
3   cups oatmeal (quick or old-fashioned)
1   cup pecan pieces (optional)
1   cup raisins

Heat oven to 350° F. Beat margarine and sugars until creamy. Add eggs and vanilla; beat well. In another bowl, combine flour, baking soda, cinnamon and salt. Add to margarine mixture; mix well. Stir in oatmeal, pecans and raisins. Mix well. Drop by rounded tablespoons onto ungreased cookie sheet. Bake 10 to 12 minutes or until golden brown. Cool 1 minute on cookie sheet, remove to wire rack. Cool completely. Store in air tight container.

Serves 6 to 8

Audrey Lyons

COCA-COLA CAKE

2   cups flour
2   cups sugar
2   sticks oleo
2   tablespoons cocoa
1   cup Coca-Cola
2   eggs
1   cup buttermilk
1   teaspoon baking soda
2   teaspoons vanilla
1 ½ cups miniature marshmallows

Combine flour and sugar. In a saucepan, heat oleo, cocoa and cola to a boil. Pour over first mixture. In a bowl, beat eggs, add buttermilk, baking soda, vanilla and marshmallows. Combine both mixtures and mix well. Pour into cake pan. Bake at 350° F for 30-35 minutes. Ice while hot.

ICING:

1   stick oleo
3   tablespoons cocoa
6   tablespoons Coca-Cola
1   16-ounce box powdered sugar
1   cup chopped nuts

Boil oleo, cocoa and cola. Pour over powdered sugar; mix well. Add nuts. Pour over cake, spread evenly.

NOTE: Use a king size Coke. After the cup of Coke is used for the cake the remainder will measure 6 tablespoons.

Serves 6 to 8

Peggy Favre

Brittany and Jade enjoy birthday cake.

153

STRAWBERRY DELIGHT

1 ½ cups flour
2 tablespoons confectioner's sugar
1 ½ sticks margarine
¾ cup pecans, chopped
1 8-ounce package cream cheese, softened
¼ cup granulated sugar
2 tablespoons milk
3 ½ cups cool whip
2 pints strawberries, halved
2 ½ cups cold milk
1 6-ounce package instant vanilla pudding
Pie crust

Sift flour and confectioners sugar together. Add margarine and cut in with pastry blender. Stir in pecans and pat mixture into 9"x13" pan. Bake at 350° F for 20 minutes. Cool.

Beat cream cheese with granulated sugar and 2 tablespoons of milk, until smooth. Fold in ½ cup of cool whip. Spread over crust. Arrange strawberries in even layer.

Using 2 ½ cups of milk, mix pudding as directed on package. Pour over berries. Chill several hours or overnight.

Shortly before serving, spread remaining cool whip over pudding.

Serves 6 to 8

Debbie Lain

BRITTANY & DYLAN'S HOLIDAY COOKIES

Make basic sugar cookie dough. Use any holiday cookie molds or cookie cutters with the following decorations:

Eyes: M&M's, red hots, etc.
Nose: Candy corn, spiced gum drops, etc.
Mouth: Sliced orange jelly candies, thin red licorice strips.

Christmas Trees: M&M's, red hots, colorful sugar sprinkles, gum drops, Pez candies. The trees look great frosted in Betty Crocker vanilla frosting colored with green food coloring and decorations.

Ghost Cut-outs: Chocolate chip eyes, frosted with vanilla frosting.

We like to be creative and use many kinds of candy.

Serves 4 to 6

Brittany & Dylan Favre

BANANA PUDDING

3   small packages vanilla instant pudding
1   8-ounce container sour cream
1   large Cool Whip
6   bananas
1   box vanilla wafers

Mix pudding mix per package directions (less one cup of milk). Add sour cream and half the Cool Whip to mixture. Slice bananas and crumble half a box of vanilla wafers. Layer as follows: vanilla wafer crumbs, bananas, pudding mix. Use the remaining Cool Whip for topping. Prepare in 10" x 13" glass pan.

Note: You may substitute sugar-free pudding and low fat Cool Whip and sour cream to cut calories on this dish.

Serves 4 to 6

Gloria Jordan

MOM'S CHRISTMAS CREAM PUFFS

(We say Christmas because this is the only time we can get Mom to make them.)

½   cup butter
1   cup boiling water
1   cup all-purpose flour, sifted
¼   teaspoon salt
4   eggs
1   box vanilla pudding

Melt butter in 1 cup boiling water. Add flour and salt all at once. Stir vigorously. Cook and stir until mixture forms a ball that doesn't separate. Remove from heat; cool slightly. Add eggs, one at a time, heating after each until smooth.

Drop by heaping tablespoons 3 inches apart on ungreased cookie sheet. Bake at 450° F for 15 minutes, then at 325° F for 25 minutes. Remove from oven; split. Turn oven off; put cream puffs back in to dry, about 20 minutes. Cool on rack. Makes 10 or if you prefer, make them smaller.

Fill with vanilla pudding (I use the prepared box mix).

Serves 6 to 8

Bonita Favre

MAWMAW'S COCONUT CAKE

1   package white cake mix
1   small cool whip
1   cup sugar
2 ½ 6-ounce packages frozen coconut
8   ounces sour cream

Bake cake by directions on package, using 2 round cake pans. Mix cool whip, sugar, 2 packages coconut and sour cream. Spread icing between each layer and frost sides and top. Top with remaining coconut.

Serves 6 to 8

Mary Favre

BANANA FRITTERS

¾ cup self-rising flour
¾ cup milk
1 egg
½ teaspoon salt
1 large banana or 1 ½ small bananas
½ cup oil

Mix flour, milk, egg and salt with a fork until well blended. Cut bananas into small pieces by quartering them lengthwise and slicing thin. Fold in batter. Heat oil in skillet until hot enough for fritters to float. (Test by dropping a small portion into pan.) Drop by table-spoonfuls into oil; when golden in color, turn with slotted spatula and brown other side. Drain on paper towels. For small fritters (to serve for brunch or a coffee party) drop by teaspoonfuls.

Serve with melted butter and syrup or sprinkle with confectioner's sugar.

Serves 6 to 8

Poppa Slyvester Pagano

BANANA SPLIT CAKE

Layer 1:
2 ½ cups graham cracker crumbs
1 stick melted margarine
Mix crumbs with margarine and press into bottom of large oblong pan.

Layer 2:
1 box powdered sugar
1 egg
2 sticks margarine
½ teaspoon vanilla extract (optional)
Beat ingredients 10 minutes. Place over layer 1.

Layer 3:
3 large bananas
Slice bananas over layer 2.

Layer 4:
1 can pineapple, crushed and drained
Spread over layer 3.

Layer 5:
1 large container Cool Whip
Spread over layer 4.

Layer 6:
Pecans to taste
Maraschino cherries to taste
Garnish over layer 5.

Chill at least 1 hour before serving. Chilling longer makes it better.

Note: If eaten on a day of the week that has the letter 'd', calories don't count!

Serves 6 to 8

Linda French Wittmann

LEMON MERINGUE PIE

This recipe is dedicated to my late father-in-law, Alvin Favre. On special occasions, such as his birthday and Father's Day, I would make him a lemon pie. Once I was busy and I didn't have time to make his pie, so I bought one. He called me and asked, "Who made this pie?" I told him I did. He told me he knew I didn't. From then on I made it a point to be sure he got his homemade lemon pie.

1 ½	cups sugar
3	tablespoons cornstarch
3	tablespoons all-purpose flour
	Dash of salt
1 ½	cups hot water
3	slightly beaten egg yolks
2	tablespoons butter or margarine
½	teaspoon grated lemon peel
⅓	cup lemon juice
1	9 ½" baked pie shell, cooled

In saucepan, mix sugar, cornstarch, flour and salt. Gradually add hot water, stirring constantly. Cook and stir over high heat until mixture comes to a boil. Reduce heat; cook and stir 2 minutes longer. Remove from heat.

Stir small amount of hot mixture into egg yolks; return to hot mixture. Bring to a boil and cook 2 minutes stirring constantly. Add butter and lemon peel. Slowly add lemon juice, mixing well. Pour into pastry shell. Spread meringue over filling; seal to edge.

MERINGUE

3	egg whites
½	teaspoon vanilla
¼	teaspoon cream of tartar
6	tablespoons sugar

Beat egg whites, vanilla and cream of tartar until soft peaks form. Gradually add sugar, beating until stiff and glossy peaks form and all sugar is dissolved. Spread meringue over filling, sealing to edge of pastry. Bake at 350° F for 10-12 minutes, or until meringue is golden. Cool before cutting.

Serves 6 to 8

Bonita Favre

NEVER-FAIL DIVINITY

4   cups sugar
1   cup light corn syrup
¾   cup water
      Dash salt
3   egg whites
1   teaspoon vanilla extract
½   cup chopped pecans

Combine sugar, corn syrup, water and salt in 2-quart glass casserole dish. Microwave on high for 19 minutes, or to 260° F on candy thermometer, stirring every 5 minutes. Beat egg whites until very stiff. Pour hot syrup gradually over egg whites, beating on high speed for about 12 minutes or until thick and candy begins to lose gloss. Fold in vanilla and pecans. Drop by spoonfuls onto waxed paper. Let sit until candy is solid.

Serves 6 to 8

Bonita Favre

Kathy Roberts, Bonita and Pat Ladner having a good time making candy for Christmas.

MEEMAW FRENCH'S BREAD PUDDING

1	loaf French bread
6	eggs
1	large box raisins
1	tablespoon cinnamon
1	teaspoon nutmeg
1	tablespoon vanilla extract
½	cup brown sugar
	Milk
1	stick butter or margarine

Slice the bread thin, put in a large mixing bowl and add eggs, raisins, cinnamon, nutmeg, vanilla extract, brown sugar and enough milk to soak up bread. Soak for about 3 hours, or overnight in the refrigerator. Melt butter in a 9" x 9" pan, then pour mixture in the pan. Mix well with butter.

Scott, Brandi, Jeff, Meemaw and Brett

TOPPING:

3	tablespoons brown sugar
1	teaspoon granulated sugar
1	teaspoon cinnamon
½	teaspoon nutmeg

Mix brown sugar, sugar, cinnamon and nutmeg together and sprinkle over top. Bake for 30 minutes in 250° F oven.

BRANDY SAUCE:

1	stick butter or margarine
	sugar
1	jigger brandy

Melt butter on low heat in a saucepan. Set aside to cool. When cool, add enough sugar to absorb the cool butter. When cold, add brandy and mix. Serve over bread pudding.

Serves 6 to 8

Izella "Meemaw" French

HUMMINGBIRD CAKE

CAKE:

3 cups all-purpose flour
2 cups sugar
1 teaspoon baking soda
1 teaspoon salt
1 teaspoon ground cinnamon
3 eggs, beaten
1 cup vegetable oil
1 ½ teaspoons vanilla extract
1 8-ounce can crushed pineapple
1 cup pecans, chopped
2 cups bananas, chopped

Combine first 5 ingredients in large bowl, add eggs and oil, stirring until dry ingredients are moistened. Do not beat. Stir in vanilla, pineapple, pecans and bananas. Spoon batter into 3 greased and floured 9" round cake pans. Bake at 350° F for 25 to 30 minutes, until toothpick inserted comes out clean. Cool in pans 10 minutes, remove and cool completely. Cake is ready to be frosted. Spread frosting between each layer and frost sides and top. Sprinkle chopped pecans on top.

Monica and Christy at Mardi Gras

CREAM CHEESE FROSTING:

1 8-ounce package cream cheese
½ cup butter or margarine
1 16-ounce package powdered sugar, sifted
1 teaspoon vanilla

Combine cream cheese and butter, beating until smooth. Add powdered sugar and vanilla; beat until light and fluffy.

Serves 6 to 8

Monica Ladner Wittmann

PEANUT BUTTER COOKIES

½   cup butter
½   cup peanut butter
½   cup granulated sugar
½   cup brown sugar
1   egg
¼   cup self-rising flour

Cream together butter, peanut butter, sugars and egg. Blend in flour.
Mix all ingredients together well. Cover and chill for 30 minutes.
Heat oven to 375° F. Shape dough into 1-inch balls. Place 3 inches
apart on lightly greased baking sheet. With fork dipped into flour,
flatten balls in crisscross pattern. Bake 10-12 minutes or until set but
not hard.

Yields 3 dozen cookies

Sandy Adams

BUTTERMILK CAKE

1   cup shortening
2 ¾   cups sugar
5   eggs
⅓   teaspoon baking soda
1   tablespoon warm water
1   teaspoon vanilla
1   cup buttermilk
3   cups flour

Blend together shortening and sugar. Add in eggs one at a time. Dissolve soda in warm water, then mix it and vanilla in buttermilk. Alternate mixing in the buttermilk and egg mixture with flour. Pour into a greased and floured tube pan. Bake 1 hour at 325° F, then 30 minutes at 350° F.

Serves 6 to 8

Mary (Mawmaw) Favre

BLUEBERRY CRUNCH CAKE

1   20-ounce can crushed pineapple, undrained
3   cups blueberries
⅓   cup sugar
1   yellow cake mix
1   stick margarine, melted
¼   cup sugar
1   cup chopped pecans

Place pineapple and blueberries in a 9" x 13" baking dish. Sprinkle ⅓ cup sugar and dry cake mix over the blueberries. Pour melted margarine over the cake mix. Sprinkle ¼ cup sugar over the margarine and cake mix. Top with chopped pecans. Bake 350° F for 45 minutes.

Serves 6 to 8

Myra Marsh

My love for blueberries started about 10 years ago, when my dad planted about 10 bushes. Now he has about 150. So each year I pick about 10 gallons, and friends and family also come and pick, and enjoy them. The Blueberry Crunch Cake is my favorite. It is the dessert I take to all the parties at the Favres. It is usually gone 10-15 minutes after I get there.

- *Myra Marsh*

BLUEBERRY CRUMB MUFFINS

Note: Self-rising flour may be used; just omit baking powder and salt.

MUFFINS:

2 cups flour
3 teaspoons baking powder
½ cup sugar
½ teaspoon salt
1 ½ cups blueberries
1 egg
¼ cup oil
1 cup milk

Combine flour, baking powder, sugar, salt and blueberries. Mix egg, oil and milk together and add to the dry ingredients stirring just enough to moisten. Pour muffins into prepared muffin pan.

FOR TOPPING:

¼ cup butter
½ cup brown sugar
¼ teaspoon cinnamon
½ cup flour

For topping: Cut butter into brown sugar, cinnamon and flour. Should be meal-like. Crumble topping on each muffin.

Bake 375° F for 25 to 30 minutes.

Makes 18 medium sized muffins.

Myra Marsh

BLUEBERRY BUCKLE

Note: If you do not have buttermilk, use this substitution.
1 cup buttermilk: equals 1 tablespoon lemon juice or vinegar, and add milk to equal 1 cup. Let mixture stand for 5 minutes.

¾ cup granulated sugar
¼ cup butter
2 eggs
1 teaspoon vanilla
2 cups all-purpose flour
2 teaspoons baking powder
½ teaspoon salt
¼ teaspoon ground cinnamon
½ cup buttermilk
2 ½ cups fresh or frozen blueberries

Preheat oven to 375° F. Grease 9" square baking pan; set aside. Beat sugar and butter in large bowl with electric mixer at medium speed until well blended. Beat in eggs and vanilla. In another bowl, combine flour, baking powder, salt and cinnamon. Stir flour mixture and buttermilk alternately into sugar mixture until well blended. Stir in blueberries. Spoon batter into prepared pan. Set aside.

Streusel Topping:

¼ cup all purpose flour
¼ cup granulated sugar
¼ cup brown sugar, packed
½ teaspoon ground cinnamon
¼ cup butter or margarine

Combine flour, sugar, brown sugar and cinnamon and mix until well blended. Cut in butter with pastry blender or 2 knives until mixture resembles coarse crumbs.

Sprinkle streusel topping evenly over batter and bake 25-30 minutes or until toothpick inserted into center comes out clean.

Serves 9

Myra Marsh

OATMEAL-MACAROON-COOKIES

1 ¼	cups sifted flour
½	teaspoon salt
1	teaspoon soda
3	cups quick oats
½ to ¾	cup nuts (I use pecans)
1	cup coconut
1	cup shortening, or oleo
1	cup brown sugar
1	cup white granulated sugar
½	teaspoon vanilla
2	eggs, unbeaten

Mix flour, salt, soda, oats, nuts and coconut, and set aside.

Mix together shortening, brown sugar, sugar, vanilla and eggs. Then combine shortening and oatmeal mixtures.

Shape into walnut size ball and roll it into granulated sugar. Place on ungreased cookie sheet and bake at 350° F for 12-15 minutes.

Yields 5 dozen cookies

Louise French Green

CINNAMON NUT SOUR CREAM CAKE

Have all ingredients at room temperature.

2   sticks oleo
2   cups sugar
2   eggs
1   teaspoon vanilla flavoring
8   ounces sour cream
1   teaspoon baking powder
2   cups cake flour
1   teaspoon butter flavoring
½   cup pecans
1   teaspoon cinnamon
1   teaspoon sugar

Cream oleo and sugar. Add eggs and beat well. Add in vanilla, sour cream, baking powder and cake flour; beat 2 full minutes. Pour ½ of the batter into well greased bundt pan, add sprinkle mixture of pecans, cinnamon and sugar. Add rest of the batter and bake 55 minutes in 350° F oven.

Do not open oven door while cooking.

Serves 6 to 8

Louise French Green

BEST OF THE COAST

Because of the many tourists who visit our area, we wanted to include this chapter as a recommendation for visitors to enjoy some of our favorite eating establishments.

The Mississippi Gulf Coast is 26 miles of white sand beaches located between the cities of New Orleans and Mobile, Alabama. It is comprised of Hancock, Harrison and Jackson counties. The Gulf Coast waters offer breathtaking waterfront properties with antebellum homes, Creole cottages, massive live oak trees and a down-home environment.

The Coast always has a celebration of some sort going on. There are seafood festivals, Blessing of the Fleet, Crawfish & Crab festivals, Deep Sea Fishing Rodeos, Mardi Gras, boat races, rodeos, concerts, art shows, craft shows and many other enjoyable events.

Outdoor fun is always an adventure. With the Coast beaches, there is jet-skiing, fishing and crabbing. There are nineteen golf courses for the avid golfer, which can be played year-round.

Our newest entertainment is the emergence of the casino industry. There are presently eleven casinos from Bay St. Louis to Biloxi. They not only offer gaming fun, but great Las Vegas-style entertainment, fine hotels and great food.

We would like to extend an invitation to all our readers to visit our beautiful "Playground of the South" and enjoy some great southern hospitality.

The following pages offer the house specialties at some of our favorite Gulf Coast restaurants.

Bonita Favre

Ship Island Lighthouse

Before there was a lighthouse on Ship Island, the island had already been established as a small colony within itself.

Inbound ships loaded with supplies landed there for the Louisiana colony.

The first lighthouse was built in 1853 and was all but destroyed in the early years of the Civil War.

A new lighthouse was built in 1886 and stood until 1972 when it was accidentally burned to the ground by a couple of campers.

A new lighthouse was built in 1999 just in time to celebrate the Tricentennial of the Mississippi Gulf Coast.

LIL' RAY'S

"Since 1970, Ray Kidd has been serving up hot and spicy boiled shrimp, crabs, crawfish, fried shrimp, oysters, fish, gumbo and delicious New Orleans style po' boys. Located in Waveland, Mississippi, Lil' Ray's is a tradition for Hancock County residents and a "must stop" for people passing through.

"Although the building is not fancy, the atmosphere inside is first class. Not in dress, but in good old Southern Hospitality. The glossy lacquered picnic tables and the brightly painted walls welcome people of all ages and every walk of life. Lil' Ray's is a sure bet for a delicious, casual dining experience."

- *Southern Living* magazine

Ray Kidd and some of his reasons to smile.

DADDY RAY'S SHRIMP REMOULADE

1	pint green onions, chopped
1	quart celery, finely chopped
⅓	cup salad olives
1	pint mayonnaise
	Dash of hot sauce
1	teaspoon L&P Worcestershire sauce
2	tablespoons Creole mustard
2	tablespoons ketchup
1	hard boiled egg, minced
1	wedge lemon
12	boiled shrimp

Combine all ingredients except shrimp and mix well. Put boiled shrimp on a bed of shredded lettuce. Cover with remoulade sauce. Serve with crackers.

Serves 10 to 12

Ray Kidd

HARBOR VIEW CAFE

Harbor View Cafe is located on Highway 90-105 W. Beach Blvd., in Pass Christian, Mississippi, and is family owned and operated.

It overlooks the beautiful harbor in Pass Christian ... serving breakfast, lunch and dinner. If you visit you won't want to miss the delicious omelets, signature salads, home-made soups, fresh seafood dinner platters and sinful desserts. The gourmet coffees and cappuccino are always a favorite at the Harbor View, or cool down with a refreshing Italian soda. Now serving homemade crab cakes and steaks cooked to order Friday and Saturday evenings.

CREOLE SHRIMP OMELET

1   tablespoon butter
12 fresh shrimp
1   teaspoon onion, minced
1   teaspoon green bell pepper, minced
3   eggs
2   slices Swiss cheese
    Dash of cayenne pepper
    Dash of garlic salt
    Dash of onion salt
    Pinch of parsley

Melt butter in 10" pan. Sauté shrimp, onion and bell pepper until tender. Whisk eggs, pour into pan and cook until edges are light brown. Add cheese. Flip omelet, sprinkle with cayenne, garlic salt, onion salt and parsley. Serve with hash brown potatoes or grits.

Serves 1 to 2

Harbor View Cafe

Pass Christian Yacht Club 1950's

The Pass Christian Yacht Club is the second oldest Yacht Club in the United States. New York has the oldest. 'Nuff said about that.

The old building was an 1800's vintage home prior to the time the P.C.Y.C. acquired it as their new location. It served in that capacity for four or five years, and was demolished to make way for lanes added to U.S. Highway 90.

The club was relocated on the southeastern tip of the Pass Harbor in the fifties. In 1969 hurricane Camille destroyed it and a new one was built on the same spot where it remains today.

JOCELYN'S RESTAURANT
OCEAN SPRINGS, MISSISSIPPI

Located on Highway 90, Jocelyn's Restaurant is family owned and operated and specializes in seafood and catering. The Favre family celebrated the christening of Jade Favre, son of Jeff Favre, along with Bishop Joseph Howze and Fr. Schneider at Jocelyn's.

ASPARAGUS CASSEROLE

1	cup Ritz crackers, crushed
2	14-ounce cans cut asparagus
1	cup sharp grated cheese
1	egg, beaten
½	cup milk
½	cup melted butter
	Salt to taste
	Pepper to taste

Bishop Joseph Howse and Fr. Schneider join the Favre feast at Jocelyn's.

Line casserole dish with layer of crushed crackers leaving some for the top. Add asparagus and cheese. Mix egg, milk and melted butter with salt and pepper. Pour half the mixture over asparagus and cover with remaining crackers. Pour remaining sauce over top layer. Bake 1 hour at 350° F.

Serves 6 to 8

Jocelyn's Restaurant

JACKIE O'S CAFE
DIAMONDHEAD, MISSISSIPPI

Jackie O's is especially known for serving home cooked meals with lots of southern hospitality.

SHRIMP CREOLE

1 stick butter
3 pounds raw shrimp, peeled
 Dash salt
 Dash cayenne pepper
3 cups Creole sauce (recipe following)
3 cups hot cooked rice

Heat butter and sauté shrimp with salt and cayenne pepper until shrimp becomes firm. Add Creole sauce and simmer together for 20 minutes. Serve with Creole sauce and rice

CREOLE SAUCE:

2 tablespoons butter
1 cup onion, chopped
1 cup bell pepper, chopped
3 cups tomato pulp, chopped
¼ teaspoon dried thyme
2 bay leaves
4 cloves garlic, minced
2 tablespoons parsley, minced
1 teaspoon paprika
 Salt to taste
 Cayenne pepper to taste
1 tablespoon cornstarch
1 ½ teaspoons water

Melt butter and sauté onion and bell pepper until they become limp. Add in tomato pulp, thyme, bay leaves, garlic, parsley and paprika. Season to taste with salt and cayenne pepper. Simmer for 20 minutes.

Mix cornstarch with water and blend into the sauce. Cook for a few minutes more to thicken.

Serves 6 to 8

Jackie O's Cafe

CAJUN COUNTRY PORK SAUTACHE

1	pound lean ground pork
½	cup onion, chopped
½	cup celery, chopped
¼	cup red bell pepper, chopped
1	clove garlic, minced
½	teaspoon salt
¼	teaspoon cayenne pepper
1	8-ounce package cream cheese
2	tablespoons green onions, chopped
2	tablespoons parsley, chopped
1	8-ounce can refrigerated crescent rolls
1	egg, beaten

Brown pork; drain. Add onion, celery, bell pepper, garlic, salt and cayenne. Cook over low heat for 5 minutes. Add cream cheese, green onions and parsley. Stir until cream cheese is melted. Unroll dough on lightly greased cookie sheet; firmly press perforations to seal and spread out. Spoon pork down center leaving about 1" on both sides. Cut dough on each side in diagonal strips, fold over top. Brush dough with egg. Bake 350° F for 25-35 minutes or until golden brown.

Serves 6 to 8

Jackie O's Cafe

SHRIMP OR CRAWFISH CREAM SAUCE

½   pound margarine
1   cup onion powder
⅓   cup garlic powder
3   quarts hot water
3   pounds shrimp or crawfish tails
2   tablespoons salt
2   tablespoons pepper
½   cup parsley flakes
1   quart heavy whipping cream
     Flour
     Water

Melt margarine in medium to large pot. Take off heat. Add onion powder and garlic powder. Mix well. Add hot water and stir well. Put on medium to high heat, then add shrimp. Add salt and pepper. Mix well and add parsley flakes. Cook for 15 minutes. Add whipping cream and cook for 15 minutes. Thicken with flour and water until creamy. Serve over pasta, fried catfish, chicken or soft shell crabs.

Serves 10 to 12

Jackie O's Cafe

Alvin and Mary Favre with Chappy on their 50th wedding anniversary.

CHAPPY'S

Chappy's Seafood Restaurant is located on Highway 90, overlooking the gulf in Long Beach, Mississippi. Our grandparents, Alvin and Mary Favre, and family celebrated their 50th wedding anniversary at Chappy's.

SHRIMP ETOUFFEE

Note: You may substitute crawfish for the shrimp and make this dish as crawfish etouffee.

½   pound butter
1   cup all-purpose flour
1   large onion, chopped
1   cup green bell pepper, chopped
2   stalks celery, chopped
2 ½ quarts chicken stock
4   cups boiled shrimp
    Juice of 1 lemon
2   teaspoons garlic powder
1   teaspoon Tony Chachere's Creole Seasoning
1 ½ teaspoons cayenne pepper
1   teaspoon salt
1   teaspoon black pepper
4   cups cooked rice
    Parsley sprigs
    Green onions, chopped

In a large pot, melt butter on high heat. Add flour slowly and continue to stir until a peanut brown color, approximately 10 minutes. Add onion, bell pepper and celery to roux. Continue stirring. Slowly add chicken stock to the mixture. Mix thoroughly for 5 minutes. Add shrimp and cook for 10 minutes longer. Add lemon juice. Lower heat and cook for 30 minutes. Add in garlic powder, Tony Chachere's Seasoning, cayenne pepper, salt and pepper. Ladle over hot cooked rice. Garnish with parsley sprigs and green onions.

Serves 10 to 12

John Chapman

176

MARY'S DRIVE INN

Everything on the menu is served all of the time. Our family became patrons of Mary's many years ago when Dad and his old buddy and manager, Mr. Tony Bertucci, were coaching American Legion Baseball. It was Mr. Tony who introduced us to our favorite, crabmeat and cheese po' boys. When we are in Biloxi or have out-of-towners visiting, we are sure to make Mary's a must!

MARY'S CRABMEAT DRESSING
(FOR STUFFED CRABS & PO' BOYS)

2	tablespoons pure vegetable oil
1	cup green bell pepper, finely diced
1	cup celery, finely diced
6	cups yellow onions, finely diced
2	cups green onions, finely diced
1	bulb fresh garlic, crushed
1	tablespoon salt
1	tablespoon black pepper
2	tablespoons garlic, granulated
1	tablespoon Louisiana hot sauce
2	pounds fresh claw crabmeat, squeezed and checked for small pieces of shells
1	cup cracker meal
½	cup fine French bread crumbs

Place vegetable oil in an 8-quart pot and heat. Add green pepper and celery and sauté for 2 to 3 minutes. Add onions, green onions, fresh garlic, salt, pepper, granulated garlic and hot sauce. Sauté vegetables until yellow onions are clear. Stir occasionally. Remove from heat and let cool for 15 to 20 minutes. Add fresh claw meat to mixture and mix well. (We use our hands.) Add cracker meal and bread crumbs and mix well. At this point the dressing should be of a sticky consistency. If still wet or soggy, add more bread crumbs. Dressing is best if refrigerated overnight.

When ready to make stuffed crabs or po' boys, oil skillet or griddle with light butter and pat dressing flat on surface. Brown on both sides. Now, you can stuff your crabshells or place on po' boy bread and dress with mayonnaise, lettuce and tomatoes (cheese is optional, but delicious). Pressed on po' boy press until bread is toasted and cheese is melted.

Serves 6 to 8

Mary's Drive Inn

TRAPANI'S

Trapani's is located in the old town of Bay St. Louis, which is known for all it's great antique shopping.

FRIED SPECKLED TROUT WITH CRAWFISH ETOUFEE

FISH:

1	egg
1	cup milk
8	8-ounce fillets speckled trout
1	tablespoon salt
1	tablespoon pepper

ETOUFFEE:

1	pound butter
2	cups flour
2	cups celery, chopped
2	cups yellow onions, chopped
1 ½	cups green bell pepper, chopped
3	cloves garlic, chopped
8	bay leaves
4	cups chicken stock
1	small can Rotel tomatoes, diced
2	pounds pre-cooked crawfish tails with fat
	Salt to taste
	Pepper or Creole seasoning to taste

Combine egg and milk and pour over trout.

Etoufee: Make a light brown roux (see page 43) with butter and flour. Add celery, onions, bell pepper, garlic and bay leaves to roux; cook until tender, about 20 minutes, stirring often. Add in chicken stock and Rotel tomatoes; simmer for 15 minutes, or until thick. Add in crawfish tails, salt, pepper or Creole seasoning. Continue to simmer while frying fish.

Mix together the fish fry, salt and pepper. Dip fish in fish fry mixture and deep fry at 350° F until golden brown. Place on platter and top with crawfish.

Serves 8

Anthony Trapani III

BEST OF THE REST

My family's restaurant legacy began in New Orleans in 1946. An unusual passion for food and a burning determination to succeed brought my grandfather, Owen Patrick Brennan, father, Dick Brennan and his siblings great success, which soon put our restaurant and our family "on the map." This overwhelming success created a restaurant empire known for utilizing quality local ingredients, providing first-rate service and serving as a nurturing ground for some of the most well-known chefs in the country, including Paul Prudhomme and Emeril Lagasse. Our philosophy is timeless. Every person who enters our restaurants is as important as a guest entering our own home, since for us the restaurants are an extension of our home.

At home is where my love of cooking first began at a very young age. Having grown up the son of legendary restaurateur Dick Brennan, the restaurant business was not just a part of life for me, it was a way of life. A way of life that has always consisted of what we call the basics - food, family, friends and fun.

The luck of the Irish being on our side, my family has been fortunate enough to be united with another family who cherishes the same basics of food, family, friends and fun - the Favres. Their family home is conveniently located across Rotten Bayou (or as we call it, the "Au Gratin" bayou) from our family's summer home, Brenwood. Being close enough to shout family recipes across the water, the Favre family home has served as the backdrop for many backyard celebrations complete with plenty of great food, good friends, lots of family and tons of fun.

It has been a super experience getting to know the Favres and working with them on their family cookbook. We hope the stories and the recipes add as much revelry to your family's next festive occasion as we had compiling the information for the book. We like to think of it as "Cooking with Jazz" bayou-style!

Dickie Brennan

(Painting by Marilyn Carter Rougelot)

Dickie Brennan
(Photo by Kurt Coste)

179

Dickie Brennan & Co
A RESTAURANT GROUP

CHEFS

Palace Cafe:
Gus Martin

Dickie Brennan's Steakhouse:
James Leeming

Mr. B's Bistro:
Michelle McRaney

THE BRENNANS

Here is a chapter we cannot say enough about. You see, the Favre name has not always been as well-known as it is today. The Brennan name has been famous in the restaurant business for a long time, not only in New Orleans, but all over the country, and for good reason. The descendants of Owen Patrick Brennan are known for creating some of the best food ever served. I speak from experience. All you have to do is try some of their recipes and you'll agree.

I have had the privilege and honor to spend some time with Dick Brennan and his son Dickie. (A special thanks for the help and the time they have given on development of this book.) They are some of the finest people on the planet. I should also mention that they are our neighbors across the Rotten Bayou in the house of the late Charlie Cantrell, the former owner of Pat O'Brien's in New Orleans. If they aren't hard at work in New Orleans making thousands of people happy by introducing them to some of the best cuisine known to mankind, they are gathering on the banks of the Rotten Bayou enjoying the four F's. As Dickie said mid-morning on Labor Day, "this is what it is all about ... friends and family gathering to share some good food and good times."

Dickie Brennan's Steakhouse, Palace Café, and Mr. B's Bistro are located in the French Quarter in New Orleans.

Jeff Favre

Jeff Favre and Dick Brennan

HOUSE FILET

6   ounces creamed spinach (see page 182)
4   ounces Pontalba Potatoes (see page 183)
1   8-ounce beef filet, cooked to desired temperature
1 ½ ounces Béarnaise Sauce (recipe following)
5   fresh oysters, fried golden brown

Spread Creamed Spinach across the entire bottom of a plate, in a circle. Place Pontalba Potatoes in small circle in center of plate. Place filet on top of the potatoes. Ladle the Béarnaise sauce over the filet. Place fried oysters around the filet.

BÉARNAISE SAUCE:

4   tablespoons fresh tarragon, chopped
½   gallon hollandaise sauce

To make Béarnaise sauce: Fold tarragon into hollandaise sauce; set aside.

Serves 1

DICKIE BRENNAN'S
Steakhouse

DICKIE BRENNAN'S
Steakhouse

CREAMED SPINACH

1	tablespoon unsalted butter
3	ounces yellow onion, sliced
12	ounces fresh spinach, picked clean
½	cup Béchamel sauce (see recipe following)
¼	cup heavy cream
	Creole seasoning to taste

In sauté pan, melt butter. Add onions and fresh spinach and sauté until wilted. Add Béchamel sauce and heavy cream and stir. Season to taste with Creole seasoning. Serve immediately in a dip dish.

Serves 2

BÉCHAMEL SAUCE:

2	ounces unsalted butter
2	ounces all-purpose flour
1	cup whole milk
4	ounces yellow onion, chopped
1	bay leaf
2	whole cloves
	Kosher salt to taste
	White pepper to taste

In medium size pan, melt butter. Add flour and make a white roux by whisking thoroughly. In medium sauce pot, combine milk, onion, bay leaf, cloves, salt and pepper; bring to a simmer over low heat. Slowly add white roux by whisking it in, and allowing sauce to thicken. Strain sauce, set aside to cool and then add to spinach mixture.

Serves 2

PONTALBA POTATOES

1   medium potato
3   cups vegetable oil
1 ½ tablespoons unsalted butter
2   ounces yellow onion, julienne
1   ounce Tasso, diced small
½   tablespoon fresh garlic, chopped
2   ounces wild mushroom mix (shiitake, crimini, oyster, or your choice)
½   ounce green onions, finely chopped
1   tablespoon brandy
      Creole seasoning to taste

DICKIE BRENNAN'S
Steakhouse

Wash potato and bake in an oven at 350° F for 40 minutes. Cool potato, peel and cut into medium size cubes (½" x ½"). In large pot, add oil and bring to 350° F. Add potatoes and fry until golden brown (about 4 minutes). Strain and set aside over paper towels to absorb extra oil.

In sauté pan, melt butter over medium heat, add onion and cook until slightly brown. Add Tasso and garlic and cook until garlic is lightly toasted. Add mushrooms and cook until tender. Add fried potatoes, green onions, brandy and seasoning, toss to mix and serve.

Serves 1

DICKIE BRENNAN'S *Steakhouse*

CREOLE ONION SOUP

6	ounces unsalted butter
1 ½	pounds yellow onions, julienne
2	ounces, all-purpose flour
1	quart chicken stock or broth
8	ounces white wine
½	quart milk
½	quart heavy cream
2	bay leaves
2	tablespoons kosher salt
1	teaspoon white pepper, fresh ground
18	ounces Cheddar cheese, shredded

In large pot, melt butter over medium heat. Add the julienne onions and cook until translucent (do not brown). Add flour to pot and cook for 8 minutes, stirring constantly. DO NOT BROWN THE FLOUR! Add chicken stock or broth, white wine, milk, cream and bay leaves and bring to a boil. Reduce to low heat and allow soup to simmer for 20 minutes. Remove bay leaves, add salt and pepper. With a hand mixer or blender, purée soup, add Cheddar cheese slowly until dissolved. Serve immediately.

Yields 1 gallon

TOMATO-BLEU CHEESE NAPOLEON

1 ounce leaf lettuce, chiffonade
1 each crouton, slice on a bias 3 to 4 inches, toasted
2 slices tomato, ½ inch thick
2 ounces Maytag bleu cheese, crumbled
1 ounce red onion, shaved
1 ½ ounces Remoulade dressing (see recipe following)

Place chiffonade of lettuce on bottom of six-inch plate, in a rectangular shape about 1 to 1 ½ inches wide. Place crouton on the center of plate on top of lettuce. Add tomato, bleu cheese and red onion. Repeat tomato, bleu cheese and red onion. Ladle Remoulade sauce on top of dish perpendicular to lettuce.

Serves 1

REMOULADE SAUCE:

¼ cup Creole mustard
4 tablespoons Dijon mustard
3 cloves fresh garlic, chopped
1 medium yellow onion, roughly chopped
4 tablespoons fresh parsley, chopped
2 ½ cups ketchup
½ cup white vinegar
¼ cup Worcestershire sauce
1 ½ teaspoons paprika
2 stalks celery, roughly chopped
2 tablespoons salt
1 tablespoon Crystal hot sauce
3 tablespoons fresh green onions, chopped
½ teaspoon lemon zest
1 tablespoon horseradish
3 whole eggs
2 cups salad oil or vegetable oil

In large container mix all ingredients except eggs and oil. Purée all until fully incorporated. While puréeing, add eggs one by one and bind mixture. Add oil slowly to emulsify. Place in refrigerator to cool and serve atop Tomato-Bleu Cheese Napoleon. Shelf life is 3 to 4 days.

Yields 2 ½ quarts

DICKIE BRENNAN'S
Steakhouse

(Photo by Kurt Coste)

185

DICKIE BRENNAN'S
Steakhouse

PRIME BEEF TENDERLOIN

18   ounces seasoned beef tenderloin, cooked to temperature and sliced
2   ounces oil
1   teaspoon fresh garlic, chopped
4   ounces wild mushroom mix (shiitake, oyster, crimini, button - all sliced)
1   red bell pepper, roasted, cooled, peeled, julienne
1   tablespoon brandy
9   ounces Brandy Cream Sauce (recipe following)
1   teaspoon Creole seasoning
2   quarts water
12   ounces Capellini pasta

In large sauté pan, over medium - high heat, blacken beef tenderloin to desired temperature, then remove and cool in refrigerator. In a sauté pan at medium heat, add oil, then garlic. Lightly toast the garlic, and add wild mushroom mix. Then add the julienne roasted peppers and sauté until tender. Add sliced beef, then remove pan from fire and add brandy, carefully return to fire and flame it. Add the Brandy Cream Sauce and bring to a boil. Add Creole seasoning to season mixture.

In large pot, bring 2 quarts of water to a boil, and cook pasta al dente. Remove and drain. Plate the pasta splitting it into six portions of 2 ounces each. Spoon about 3 ounces of the beef mixture over the pasta. Serve immediately.

Serves 6 appetizer size portions

BRANDY CREAM SAUCE:

2	teaspoons unsalted butter
2	tablespoons fresh shallots, chopped
1	teaspoon fresh garlic, chopped
1	tablespoon celery, diced small
1	tablespoon carrots, diced small
½	cup red wine
1	cup veal demi-glace
½	cup brandy
½	cup heavy cream
½	teaspoon salt
¼	teaspoon white pepper

In sauce pan at medium heat, melt butter, then add shallots, garlic, celery and carrots. Sauté all items until tender, then add red wine and bring mixture to a boil, and reduce it by three quarters its volume. Add veal demi-glace and brandy, bring to a boil and reduce by half its volume. Add heavy cream, bring to a boil and reduce by half its volume. At this point the sauce has gone through a natural reduction and is ready to be seasoned with salt and white pepper to taste. Strain the sauce. Add sauce to sauté pan to be used in Prime Beef Tenderloin appetizer recipe.

Yields 8 to 10 ounces

DICKIE BRENNAN'S
Steakhouse

DICKIE BRENNAN'S
Steakhouse

BANANAS FOSTER BREAD PUDDING

4   loaves French bread, each 1 foot long
1   quart heavy cream
1 ½ cups milk
1 ½ cups sugar
3   cups light brown sugar
45   egg yolks
3   bananas
1   cup rum
½   teaspoon cinnamon powder
4   tablespoons vanilla extract
½   gallon vanilla ice cream
1   bunch fresh mint
1 ¾ quarts Rum Raisin Crème Anglaise (see recipe following)

Slice the loaves of French bread and dry in an oven at 200° F for 20 minutes. In a large container, add the remaining ingredients, except ice cream, mint and Rum Raisin Crème Anglaise, and blend with a hand mixer or blender. Pour into a 8" x 10" x 2" pan, then mush all bread by hand, being sure to flatten all of the lumps. Cover pan with foil and bake at 300° F for 2 ½ hours or until a skewer can be inserted and comes out dry. Remove foil and continue baking for an additional 20 minutes or until golden brown. Cool down at room temperature. Cut into 3 ½" x 3 ½" squares. Place each piece on a plate and top with desired amount of vanilla ice cream. Then ladle about ½ cup of Rum Raisin Crème Anglaise over the ice cream and garnish with a mint leaf.

Serves 18

Rum Raisin Crème Anglaise:

1 ½ cups sugar
½ quart heavy cream
10 egg yolks
1 cup rum
8 ounces dark raisins

In large sauce pot bring sugar and cream to a boil. In separate container with egg yolks, add the cream-sugar mixture slowly, stirring vigorously to temper sugared yolks without scrambling them. Once yolks have been tempered, return cream-sugar mixture to stove. Reduce fire to low, and stir mixture constantly until sauce thickens or until it covers the back of a wooden spoon. Strain through a fine strainer into a large container, and place in refrigerator until cool.

In large sauté pan, cook rum and raisins over medium heat, until alcohol has evaporated. Watch out for the flame! Place in refrigerator until cooled. Once cooled add to Crème Anglaise while stirring. You may add or omit rum from recipe, depending on taste.

Yields 1 ¾ quarts

DICKIE BRENNAN'S
Steakhouse

OYSTER PAN ROAST

1   quart heavy cream, seasoned to taste with salt and pepper
1   tablespoon rosemary, minced
20   oysters, shucked
4   tablespoons bread crumbs
2   tablespoons Parmesan cheese
1   tablespoon parsley, chopped
4   1-ounce pieces French bread, cut on a bias
1   tablespoon butter
     Salt to taste
     Pepper to taste

Preheat oven to 350° F. In a 2-quart saucepan, reduce heavy cream by ¼ and add rosemary. Add 3 ounces cream and 5 oysters to each of 4 individual size skillets. Place each skillet on the stovetop and bring to a boil. Remove from heat. Sprinkle breadcrumbs and Parmesan cheese over each oyster. Place a French bread crouton in the center of each skillet and place back in the oven for 2 minutes. Garnish with chopped parsley.

To make French bread croutons: Cut bread on a bias. Brush both sides of each piece with melted butter, season to taste with salt and pepper, and toast in a 350° F oven until crisp.

Serves 4

Dickie Brennan's
PALACE Café

(Photo by Eugenia Uhl)

CATFISH PECAN MEUNIÈRE

CATFISH FILLETS:

6   7-ounce catfish fillets
2   tablespoons Creole seasoning
3   large eggs
½   cup milk
1   cup flour
1   cup Spicy Pecans (see recipe following)
1   cup Pecan Flour (see recipe following)
16   ounces Creole Meunière sauce (see recipe following)
2   ounces olive oil

Preheat oven to 350° F. Trim fat and any rough edges off the catfish fillets. Lightly season with 1 tablespoon of Creole seasoning and place in refrigerator. In a medium bowl, make an egg wash by whipping eggs and milk together. In a separate bowl, combine flour and 1 tablespoon Creole seasoning and mix well. Prepare Pecan Flour and Spicy Pecans (see recipes).

Set up a "breading station" on a table or counter top. Bread seasoned catfish fillets by first dusting them lightly in seasoned flour. Shake off any excess flour. Then place each in the egg mixture. Place the fillets in the Pecan Flour and press flour firmly against catfish until well coated.

Cover the bottom of a large skillet or sauté pan with olive oil approximately ⅛" deep and heat until hot but not smoking. Gently place fish into the hot oil. Cook 4 to 5 minutes until lightly browned. Gently turn fillet being careful not to break the pecan crust. Continue cooking another 3 to 4 minutes until thoroughly browned. Remove fillet to a shallow baking pan and finish cooking in an oven at 450° F until done (approximately an additional 5 to 8 minutes). Place on serving plates, spoon Meunière Sauce over the fillets to desired amount and garnish with Spicy Pecans.

Serves 6

Dickie Brennan's
PALACE
Café

Dickie Brennan's

PALACE café

PECAN FLOUR:

½   cup pecans
½   cup flour
1   tablespoon Creole seasoning

Purée pecans in Cuisinart. Add flour and Creole seasoning and blend well.

SPICY PECANS:

1   cup pecans
1   ounce butter
1   tablespoon Creole seasoning
1   tablespoon sugar

Combine pecans, butter, Creole seasoning and sugar. Evenly lay pecans on baking sheet pan and roast 5 to 8 minutes at 350° F until lightly browned.

CREOLE MEUNIÈRE SAUCE:

1   lemon, peeled and quartered
½   cup Worcestershire sauce
½   cup Crystal hot sauce
¼   cup heavy whipping cream
1   pound cold unsalted butter, cut into small cubes
¼   teaspoon kosher salt
⅛   teaspoon white pepper

In medium sauce pot, combine lemon, Worcestershire, hot sauce and cream and reduce over medium heat. Stir constantly with a wire whisk until mixture becomes thick and syrupy. Reduce heat to low and slowly blend in butter one cube at a time. (This process is called mounting the butter.) As you add the last of the butter, remove from heat and continue to stir. Add salt and pepper to taste. Strain through a fine strainer. Serve or cover and keep sauce warm.

Serves 6

CRABMEAT CHEESECAKE WITH PECAN CRUST

Dickie Brennan's
PALACE
café

PECAN CRUST:

¾   cup pecans
1   cup flour
½   teaspoon salt
5   tablespoons cold butter
3   tablespoons ice water

Preparing the Pecan Crust:
Grind pecans, flour and salt in the food processor until fine. Transfer to a bowl. Add butter. Work the butter into the flour until you have crumbs about the size of a pea. Toss in the ice water, lifting the dough up with your fingers to evenly incorporate. The dough will remain fairly crumbly. Roll out dough on a lightly floured surface about ⅛" thick. Lightly grease the tart pan. Starting with the sides and then the bottom, press the dough into the tart pan. Bake the crust in a 350° F oven for about 20 minutes. Meanwhile, make the filling.

FILLING:

½   small onion, finely diced
2   tablespoons butter
4   ounces crabmeat, shell removed
8   ounces cream cheese, room temperature
⅓   cup Creole cream cheese, or sour cream
2   eggs
      Kosher salt to taste
      White pepper to taste
      Hot sauce to taste

Preparing the Filling:
Cook the onion in butter over medium heat until translucent. Add the crabmeat and cook until just heated through. Set this aside. In a mixer fitted with a paddle, or by hand using a wooden spoon, blend the cream cheese until smooth. Add the Creole cream cheese and then the eggs one at a time. Fold in the crabmeat mixture. Season to your liking with salt, white pepper and hot sauce. Pour the mix into the prepared crust. Bake at 300° F for about 30 minutes until set and firm to the touch.

CRABMEAT CHEESECAKE WITH PECAN CRUST CONTINUED

GARNISH:

4   ounces mixed wild mushrooms, sliced
3   tablespoons soft unsalted butter
24   crab claw fingers
16   ounces Meunière Sauce (see below)
     Kosher salt to taste
     Pepper to taste

Preparing the Garnish Topping:
In separate sauté pan add butter and sauté mushrooms until tender.
Add crab claws and heat until warm. Stir the mushrooms into previ-
ously prepared Meunière sauce. Each slice of cheesecake gets three
crab claws and two tablespoons of Meunière sauce. Add salt and pepper to taste.

MEUNIÈRE SAUCE:

1   lemon, peeled and quartered
½   cup Worcestershire sauce
½   cup Crystal hot sauce
¼   cup heavy whipping cream
1   pound cold unsalted butter, cut into small cubes
¼   teaspoon kosher salt
⅛   teaspoon white pepper

Preparing the Meunière Sauce:
In medium sauce pot, combine lemon, Worcestershire, hot sauce and
cream and reduce over medium heat. Stir constantly with a wire
whisk until mixture becomes thick and syrupy. Reduce heat to low
and slowly blend in butter one cube at a time. (This process is called
mounting the butter.) As you add the last of the butter, remove from
heat and continue to stir. Add salt and pepper to taste. Strain
through a fine strainer. Serve or cover and keep sauce warm.

Yields one 9" tart

SHRIMP TCHEFUNCTE

RICE PILAF:

2   ounces butter
1   medium onion, diced
3   cups converted rice
6   cups chicken stock
3   tablespoons ice water (optional)

Heat 5-quart sauce pan, melt butter, add onion and rice. Brown rice and onion on high heat, stirring constantly. If pan gets too hot, add in ice water a tablespoon at a time to cool. Add chicken stock and bring to a boil. Stir, reduce heat to low and let simmer covered for approximately 20 minutes. Check for firmness, uncover and let sit for 10 minutes.

MEUNIÈRE SAUCE:

1   lemon, peeled and quartered
½   cup Worcestershire sauce
½   cup Crystal hot sauce
¼   cup heavy whipping cream
1   pound cold unsalted butter, cut into small cubes
¼   teaspoon kosher salt
⅛   teaspoon white pepper

In medium sauce pot, combine lemon, Worcestershire, hot sauce and cream and reduce over medium heat. Stir constantly with a wire whisk until mixture becomes thick and syrupy. Reduce heat to low and slowly blend in butter one cube at a time. (This process is called mounting butter.) As you add the last of the butter, remove from heat and continue to stir. Add salt and pepper to taste. Strain through a fine strainer. Serve or cover and keep sauce warm.

Dickie Brennan's
PALACE
café

195

SHRIMP TCHEFUNCTE CONTINUED

SAUTÉED SHRIMP:

60 medium to large shrimp
6 teaspoons butter
3 cups green onions
3 cups domestic mushrooms
Salt to taste
Pepper to taste

Wash shrimp in cold water and drain, then season shrimp with salt and pepper. Melt butter in medium sauté pan. Add shrimp, green onions and mushrooms. Cook over medium heat for 3 to 4 minutes, stirring constantly until shrimp turn pink. When ready to serve, add Meunière sauce and heat.

Pack rice in a cup (shallow coffee cup will work fine). Invert cup over corner of plate, lift slowly. Spoon Shrimp Tchefuncte around the rice.

Serves 6 to 8

TURTLE SOUP

5	ounces butter
4	ounces all-purpose flour
½	pound veal stew meat, ground
½	pound beef stew meat, ground
½	pound turtle meat, ground
1	teaspoon garlic, minced
1	tablespoon dried thyme
½	cup green pepper, minced
½	cup onion, minced
½	cup celery, minced
3	ounces tomato purée
10 ½	cups stock (preferably dark veal stock)
1	hard boiled egg, diced
½	cup spinach, cleaned and chopped
¼	cup lemon juice
½	cup sherry
2	ounces Worcestershire sauce
2	ounces Crystal hot sauce
	Salt to taste
	Fresh ground black pepper to taste

In small saucepan, prepare a blond roux by gently melting 4 ounces of butter and adding the flour. Stir the butter and flour over medium heat for 3 minutes until mixture has a pleasant toasty smell. Remove from heat, let cool and set aside.

Brown veal, beef and turtle meat in a large soup pot. Drain and set aside. In the same pot, add 1 ounce butter, garlic, thyme, green peppers, onions and celery. Cook for about 2 minutes over medium heat, stirring occasionally until vegetables are tender. Add meats and tomato purée and simmer for an additional 5 minutes. Add stock and bring to a boil. Stirring with a wire whisk, slowly add roux a little at a time, crumbling with your fingers as to avoid any lumping. Continue stirring and return to a boil. Reduce heat and simmer for 1 hour, occasionally skimming the fat that accumulates on the surface. Add remaining ingredients and simmer for an additional 20 minutes. Season to taste and serve.

Serves 12

Dickie Brennan's
PALACE
café

WHITE CHOCOLATE BREAD PUDDING

6	cups whipping cream
2	cups milk
1	cup sugar
20	ounces white chocolate (broken into small pieces)
4	whole eggs
15	egg yolks
24"	loaf of French bread (use sliced stale bread or slice bread dried in a 275° F oven)

Note: You will need 1 ounce dark chocolate for garnish. Grate the chocolate and sprinkle on top of each serving.

Preheat oven to 350° F. In large sauce pan, heat whipping cream, milk, and sugar over medium heat. When hot, take off heat and add white chocolate pieces. Stir until melted.

Combine whole eggs and egg yolks in large bowl. Slowly pour hot cream mixture into eggs in a steady stream, whipping the eggs as you pour.

Place the stale sliced bread in the pan. Pour ½ the bread pudding mix over the bread. Use your fingers to press the bread into the mix so that it absorbs the liquid and becomes soggy. Pour in remaining mix.

Cover pan with aluminum foil and bake in a 350° F oven for 1 hour. Take off foil and continue to bake for an additional ½ hour until it is set and golden brown.

White Chocolate Sauce:

½ cup whipping cream
8 ounces white chocolate (broken into small pieces)

Bring cream to a boil in a small saucepan. Remove from heat and add white chocolate. Stir until smooth and completely melted. Spoon over bread pudding.

You can either serve the bread pudding warm, spooned right out of the pan with the sauce and chocolate sprinkles, or cut into triangles like we do at the restaurant.

To make triangles:
Chill the bread pudding until set and firm (6 to 8 hours). Loosen the sides from the pan with a knife and invert the bread pudding onto a cutting surface. Cut into 6, 4 ½" x 4" squares. Cut squares in half to make 12 triangles. Place the triangles on a cookie sheet and heat in a 275° F oven for 15 minutes. Serve with sauce and garnish with dark chocolate sprinkles.

Serves 12

Makes a 12" x 9" x 2" pan

PROFITEROLES WITH
VANILLA ICE CREAM & CHOCOLATE SAUCE

PUFF PASTRY:

1	cup milk
1	cup water
½	teaspoon salt
1	tablespoon sugar
½	pound unsalted butter
2	cups flour
8	eggs
1	quart vanilla ice cream

Bring milk, water, salt, sugar and butter to a rapid boil. Add flour and stir with wooden spoon until dough comes away from the side of the pan.

Place dough in mixing bowl. Add one egg at a time until all eggs are incorporated. Pipe onto parchment paper. Bake at 400° F until golden brown.

Coat the bottom of a 9" plate with the chocolate sauce. Place the bottom half of a puff pastry and a scoop of vanilla ice cream on top of the sauce. Put the remaining half of pastry on top and garnish with more sauce and a sprinkle of powdered sugar.

Chocolate Sauce:

½   cup heavy cream
3   tablespoons sweet butter - cut into pieces
½   cup granulated sugar
⅓   cup dark brown sugar
½   cup sifted cocoa powder
¼   cup strong coffee
     Pinch salt

Place cream and butter in 1-quart saucepan over moderate heat, stir until butter melts and cream starts to boil. Add both sugars, stirring until dissolved.

Reduce heat, add salt and cocoa, and whisk until smooth. Remove from heat and thin sauce by adding coffee. Serve warm or at room temperature.

Serves 8

PASTA JAMBALAYA

1 ½ ounces andouille sausage
1 ounce cooked duck breast
1 ounce raw chicken breast, sliced thin
3 pounds (21-25 count per pound) shrimp
2 tablespoons onion, diced
½ teaspoon garlic, chopped
2 tablespoons red and green peppers, diced
½ ounce melted butter (to sauté)
3 ounces veal stock
2 tablespoons ripe tomatoes
½ teaspoon Creole seasoning
2 ½ ounces cold sweet butter pieces
4 ounces spinach fettuccine, cooked
Pinch red pepper flakes

Add andouille, duck meat, chicken breast, shrimp, onion, garlic, and peppers to hot sauté pan with melted butter. Sauté over high flame, stirring with fork and shaking pan. When shrimp are half cooked through (about 2 minutes), add veal stock, tomatoes and seasonings. Continue cooking until mixture is reduced by ⅓.

Swirl in cold butter pieces, continuously stirring with fork and rotating sauté pan until all butter is incorporated (sauce should be smooth and light). Place warm pasta in bowl, pour jambalaya over top and serve immediately.

Serves 8 to 10

MR. B'S GUMBO YAYA

½ cup oil
½ cup flour
1 ½ pounds andouille sausage
2 cups onions
¼ cup green bell peppers, chopped
¼ cup red bell peppers, chopped
1 cup celery, chopped
1 cup crushed tomatoes
3 tablespoons butter
1 teaspoon black pepper
1 teaspoon crushed red pepper
1 tablespoon garlic, chopped
1 tablespoon Creole seasoning
1 teaspoon chili pepper
1 teaspoon thyme
2 gallons chicken stock
1 cup roasted chicken
  Salt to taste

To make roux, heat oil in saucepan. Add flour and cook until flour turns a dark brown. Set aside.

In separate saucepan, sauté andouille sausage, onions, green and red peppers, celery and tomatoes in butter for approximately 10 minutes. Incorporate roux and seasonings and let simmer for 20 minutes. Slowly stir in chicken stock and simmer for 1 to 1 ½ hours. Adjust with water or chicken stock to taste. Add chicken, and then serve over hot rice.

Yields 1 - 1 ½ gallons

KILN

Located approximately ten miles north of the Mississippi Gulf Coast lies a unique community known as Kiln, Mississippi, (pronounced "Kill" and often, "The Kiln").

Its history, tradition, and heritage is as timeless as its earliest inhabitants, the Choctaw and Muskhogean Indian tribes and early white settlers who extolled its pristine beauty and bountiful resources.

Kiln derived its name in 1813 from its primary economy based upon the coal, tar and brick kilns which supplied resin mills, shingle mills and ship yards. For this reason, the term was used by the people as "I am going to 'The Kiln,' " meaning that they were going to check their kilns.

Kiln's strategic location and elevated land mass served as an ideal port for commercial transportation along the Jourdan River to other ports and industries.

By the early twentieth century Kiln experienced a unprecedented growth as it held a place of prominence in the economic, social, cultural and educational opportunities.

The beginning of the Great Depression in October, 1929, and the closing of the Edward Hines Lumber Company, the second largest and one of the most modern in the United States, in February, 1930, left the area in economic decline. The population of approximately 2,700 people dwindled to several hundred by the 1960s.

Kiln has been known for many of its native sons who have distinguished themselves in the political, professional, vocational and athletic arenas. History has recorded the excellence by which each has been so honored. (Brett Favre would be one example.)

Today, Kiln and surrounding areas are once again enjoying a period of growth which demonstrates the resourcefulness and tradition possessed by its citizens who proudly attest to being from "The Kiln."

The Broke Spoke
Kiln, MS

Steve and Mabel Haas have for many years enjoyed their little tavern in Kiln, Mississippi. It wasn't a high-profile establishment by any means. That is, until 1997, when a local hero led his football team, the Green Bay Packers, to the Super Bowl in New Orleans.

The individuals who have so kindly contributed the recipes to this publication hope that you will enjoy them as much as the generations in the past and the family and friends that continue to prepare them today.

Jay Larry Ladner

Brett Favre and the "The Pack" were gearing up to play the New England Patriots for the World Championship just 60 miles from his childhood home.

No game tickets were available and accommodations were scarce from New Orleans to Biloxi. Yet they came. The fans, they came from everywhere. Hungry for the world title and a chance to see where their All-Pro quarterback had grown up.

Needing a place to gather and celebrate, they found The Broke Spoke, right in the heart of Kiln. This tiny little watering hole, just a stone's throw from the town's blinking caution light, accommodated more than 5,000 fans that Super Bowl weekend.

Andy is a trained French chef, having served an apprenticeship under Master Chef Fernando Oca (Le Cordon Bleu, Paris). Lee is an award winning elementary teacher and has become Rooster's official Madam Ambassador. Andy loves the classical manner of cooking. However, after Lee introduced him to her grandmother, NiNi, and her mother, Gaynell, in 1961, it was a whole new ballgame. Andy quickly fell in love with Haute Acadian (High Cajun) and also Goat Acadian (Low Cajun). NiNi was born in Erath Louisiana pronounced (E-Rat). Lee is kissin' cousin to the late Dudley J. LeBlanc, perhaps the most famous of all Cajuns and founder of Hadacol...that wonderful elixir that warmed the soul of many teetotalers, with it's 18% alcohol. We feel our food is a mixture of classical French, High Cajun and just a little Low Cajun to give it "heart."

ROOSTER'S

We moved to Kiln on the Fourth of July, 1981, from Lake Charles, Louisiana. July 17th was the official birthday for Rooster's and it was dubbed the "Olde Rooster Delicatessen." It was a pitiful site then, and shows just how dangerous a mid-life crisis can be. Nevertheless, we had done it and that was that. The little restaurant which was the small front dining room with only room for twelve, a tiny area designated as a service station (2 pumps), a large room for storage and auto repairs, a grease rack and wash area for cars and two outdoor toilets. This little hodgepodge turned out to be a perfect solution to prevent a dull and humdrum retirement.

After 15 years of hard work, the small cafe has become our front dining room used mainly for our lunch crowd, and as a waiting area for our lunch crowd, and as a waiting area for the weekends. The service station and grease rack area, after a stint as a convenience store, has become our lounge and glassed-in porch. Our large storage area and auto repair shop has become our beautiful Acadian Room. We have live entertainment in there and in our lounge on weekends.

And our "outdoor toilets" have long since been moved inside.

Andy & Lee Lott

ROOSTER'S
POTATO BACON SOUP

1	pound butter
20	pieces bacon, sliced 1" wide
3	onions, coarsely chopped
4	green bell peppers, coarsely chopped
4	stalks celery, coarsely chopped
1	cup green onions, chopped
3	cups flour
4	quarts chicken stock
1 ½	quarts whipping cream
2	quarts boiled potatoes, diced
	Salt (optional) to taste
	Garlic powder to taste
	Red pepper to taste
	Black pepper to taste
	White pepper to taste

Melt butter in pot, add bacon, onions, bell peppers, celery and green onions; sauté. Then add flour and stir. Add chicken stock and whipping cream. Then add in potatoes, salt, garlic powder, red, black, and white pepper. When it boils for about 5 minutes, turn off to avoid breaking.

Note: If you want to kick it up a notch, add a combination of grated American cheese, chives, fried crumbled bacon bits and sour cream on top of each serving.

Serves 20 to 24

Andy and Lee Lott

ROOSTER'S FRENCH ONION SOUP

1   pound butter
5   large onions, cut in half and sliced
3   cups flour
8   quarts chicken stock
1   tablespoon cayenne pepper
1   tablespoon red pepper
1   tablespoon black pepper
1   tablespoon white pepper
1   tablespoon garlic powder
2   cups green onions
    Kitchen Bouquet, for browness

Melt butter in pot and add onions, let sauté until onions turn somewhat brownish. Add flour and stir. Add in stock, seasonings and green onions. Add in Kitchen Bouquet if needed.

CROUTONS WITH CHEESE:

1   loaf French bread
    Swiss cheese

Cut French bread into small slices, add Swiss cheese on top and lightly toast. Lay on top of soup.

Serves 30 to 34

Andy and Lee Lott

ROOSTER'S
CATFISH COURTBOUILLON

1   pound butter
3   onions, coarsely chopped
4   green bell peppers, coarsely chopped
4   stalks celery, coarsely chopped
1   cup green onions, chopped
3   cups flour
5-7 quarts chicken stock
1   can diced tomatoes
1   can Rotel tomatoes
2   can stewed tomatoes
2   cans (medium) tomato sauce
4   pounds fish, cut into 1 inch squares
½   bunch parsley, chopped
4   bay leaves
1   tablespoon thyme leaves
1   tablespoon poultry seasoning
1   tablespoon black pepper
1   tablespoon white pepper
1   tablespoon red pepper,
1   tablespoon garlic powder
    Salt to taste

Melt butter in pot; add onions, bell peppers, celery and green onions.
When sautéed down, add flour; stir together, then add about 4 quarts
chicken stock. Add all cans of tomatoes, tomato sauce, and fish.
When all added, you may need to add more chicken stock to make
thinner. Then add parsley, bay leaves, thyme leaves, poultry seasoning, black, white and red pepper and garlic powder. Don't cook too
long, or fish will fall apart. Add salt.

Serves 6 to 10

Andy and Lee Lott

Gene and Lena Mae Bennet are personal friends of the Favre family. Lena Mae would bake homemade bread for Jeff every week after religion class. Gene and Lena Mae's daughter, Robin and Jeff graduated from high school together, and are still close friends.

BENNETT CHRISTMAS PARTY

What if you asked the entire town to your house for a Christmas celebration and everybody came? In Kiln, that happens each and every year at the home of Gene and Lena Mae Bennett.

It started informally (and small) in 1974 and has grown into a Christmas Eve open house for everyone. It's happening, the what, the when and where are common knowledge. No invitations are needed.

The Bennett Christmas Party is an annual event which says a lot about the way we live. We are a close-knit community. And the Bennett get-together really exemplifies that spirit during the most joyous season of the year.

It is a true Kiln tradition.

– Jeff Favre

DEER ROAST

1   large rear deer roast
1   21-ounce jar Spanish stuffed olives
2   pounds diced bacon ends and pieces
½   clove garlic, chopped
     Salt
     Pepper

Using a stiff, narrow knife, punch holes in roast approximately 1 ½" apart and almost completely through roast. Pour small amount of salt and pepper in hole, then stuff diced bacon and olives with small amounts of garlic, alternating ingredients. Stuff until holes are filled. Place on rotisserie. Cook at 350° F for four hours, or until roast shrinks on bone.

Serves 10 to 15

Gene Bennett

RED VELVET CAKE

2	1-ounce bottles red food coloring
3	tablespoons sifted cocoa
½	cup Crisco shortening
1 ½	cups sugar
2	eggs
2 ¼	cups cake flour
1	teaspoon salt
1	cup buttermilk
1	teaspoon vanilla
1	teaspoon vinegar
1	teaspoon baking soda

Mix food coloring and cocoa together. Add in shortening, sugar and eggs; cream thoroughly. Add flour and salt together, then mix buttermilk and vanilla together; alternate stirring in creamed mixture. Mix vinegar and soda together, and add to batter. Pour in cake pan, and bake at 350° F for 25 to 30 minutes.

FROSTING:

1 ½	sticks butter
12	tablespoons shortening
1 ½	cups granulated sugar
6	tablespoons flour
½	cup milk
2	teaspoons vanilla

Beat butter until fluffy. Add in shortening 1 tablespoon at a time until fluffy. Add in sugar, beating continuously. Add in flour until incorporated, then add in milk. After milk is mixed in, stir in vanilla. Frost cake after it has cooled.

Yields 2 9"cakes

Lena Mae Bennett

PECAN PRALINES

1	stick butter
3	cups sugar
	Pinch of salt
1	12-ounce can evaporated milk
2	cups pecans, chopped
1	teaspoon vanilla

Cook butter, sugar, salt and milk to soft ball stage.

Add pecans and vanilla, beat until mixture starts to thicken. Drop by spoon on wax paper. Let set up before serving.

Serves 6 to 8

Lena Mae Bennett

Growing up in Kiln, Mississippi, was a wonderful and exciting experience. That is, if Kiln is actually where we grew up. The reason I say this is because we actually didn't grow up in the heart of the Kiln. And I really don't know where we grew up. The phone book stated we lived in Fenton, but Fenton was actually 3 or 4 miles away. Our address was in Pass Christian, but Pass Christian was around 10 miles away. The area we are from consists of a bunch of small communities and towns. We were probably closer to Diamondhead than any other community or town, but it was a private community so we couldn't claim it. Delisle is the next town, but it was south of I-10, so we couldn't claim it either. The reason for that being the locals say if you live north of I-10 you are a Yankee even though we are north about 2 miles.

Therefore, since we grew up in "no mans land" and went to school in "The Kiln," we claimed it as our home. This was probably the best choice, especially since a lot of these small communities now have a Kiln address. I know I personally spent the majority of my time in Kiln and still do today. Obviously, I like it here, as do all of the Favre clan.

Jeff Favre

Maybe it's fitting since we really didn't know where we grew up that a simple task like spelling our last name correctly on a sign would prove to be difficult.

HELPFUL HINTS

Keep a few grains of rice in your salt shaker to keep it from clogging up.

To clean a build-up of burned starch on your iron, sprinkle salt on a sheet of wax paper and slide the iron back and forth. Then apply and rub in with silver polish until stain is removed.

Add a cut raw potato to food that is too salty. Discard the potato once it is boiled.

Spray new white athletic shoes heavily with starch to make them last longer.

Brush corn on the cob with a paper towel in a downward motion to remove corn silk.

Rub a bar of soap over a zipper to prevent it from sticking.

If a dish is too sweet, add salt.

To clean darkened aluminum pans, boil two teaspoons of cream of tartar mixed in a quart of water in them for about ten minutes.

To drip-dry garments faster and with fewer wrinkles, hang garments over the top of a dry cleaner's plastic bag.

Use silver polish to remove crayon marks from tile.

To draw a straighter line, use a knife instead of a pencil.

Cheese will not dry out if it is wrapped in a cloth dampened with vinegar.

Usually, very hot water will revive wilted flowers.

To cut a pie into five equal pieces, first cut a y in the pie and then two large pieces can be cut in half.

Use a damp paper towel to pick up slivered glass.

To reheat leftover rolls and biscuits, place them in paper bag which has been moistened with water. Twist the top to close and place in a hot oven until heated through.

To add shine to your hair, dilute one part apple-cider vinegar to seven parts water and rinse with it after you shampoo.

Rub mayonnaise in your hair and leave it in for five minutes to condition it. Make sure you shampoo it out thoroughly.

Fresh bread will slice better if the knife is run through a flame to heat.

Pat cooking oil on splinters. The lubrication should help it slide right out. If not, gently remove with tweezers. Splinters that are too small to get with tweezers can be removed by covering the area with white glue and letting it dry. Then peel the dried glue and the splinters go with it.

Spray garbage sacks with ammonia to prevent dogs from tearing the bags.

Cut a square from the center of a cake before slicing. This will prevent crumbling.

GLOSSARY

Al dente - Chewy.

Andouille - A Cajun smoked sausage used in cooking, made from pork with onions, garlic & cayenne pepper.

Bacon Drippings - The grease that is left after the bacon has been fried.

Baste - To keep meat from drying out while cooking, by moistening with melted butter or special sauces.

Bayou - A small body of water that flows into a river.

Beat - To mix with fast strokes until light and creamy.

Beignets - French for fritter, a doughnut type batter fried in hot oil and sprinkled with confectioners sugar.

Bisque - A highly seasoned, thick soup usually made with a cream base and shrimp, crayfish or oysters.

Blackened - A quick cooking method in a hot cast iron skillet for highly seasoned meats and fish.

Blend - To mix thoroughly two or more ingredients.

Bon Appetit - Good eating.

Boudin - A Cajun sausage made of ground pork, rice, onions and seasonings stuffed into a casing.

Butterfly - Shrimp that is sliced down the back and opened like a butterfly.

Cajun Food - South Louisiana foods cooked slowly in heavy covered pots, highly seasoned.

Cayenne Pepper - Pepper used in cooking and sauces.

Certo - A liquid sure jell - used in making jams and jellies.

Colander - A pan or basin with a perforated bottom for draining foods.

Crab boil - Seasoning used to boil crabs, shrimp and crawfish, usually found in seafood section at the store.

Crawfish - A relative of the lobster but much smaller in size.

Creole Mustard - A seasoned, prepared mustard.

Crouton - Any small piece or cube of bread that has been browned by sautéing or baking.

Emulsify - To drain out.

Dredge - To coat with dry ingredients such as flour or sugar.

Dust - To sprinkle with dry ingredients.

Etouffee - A dish made from smothering vegetables (seasoning) with seafood and cooked slowly.

Filé - A dry spice made from sassafras leaves used to thicken gumbo

Fillet - Lean deboned and skinned fish or meat, sometimes rolled or tied for cooking.

Flame - To douse with alcohol and set afire.

Green Onions - Also called scallions. The tops are used for garnishing and seasoning.

Gumbo - A soup made with a roux and stock of seafood, poultry or sausage, served over rice.

Jambalaya - A dish made from rice, meat, seafood and seasoning cooked in a pot.

Julienne - When food is cut into long, slender strips.

Marinate - To let stand in liquid.

Mince - To cut into very fine pieces.

Mirliton - A vegetable of the squash family known as a vegetable pear.

Okra - A vegetable smothered or boiled, used in gumbos. Can also be fried or pickled.

Oyster Liquor - The liquor or liquid the oysters are packed in.

Picked (in reference to crabs) - Getting all the shell off of the crab.

Pistolettes - Small individual French bread.

Po' Boy - A sandwich made with a loaf of French bread, sliced in half lengthwise and filled with meat, seafood , lettuce and tomatoes and other ingredients. A New Orleans tradition.

Praline -A candy made from cream or milk, sugar and pecans.

Redfish - Local species of red drum fish caught in the Gulf of Mexico that can be up to 30 pounds. It is usually blackened or cooked in a red gravy.

Roux - Flour and oil browned and used to thicken gumbos and stews.

Sassafras - The leaves of the sassafras tree, dried to make filé.

Sauce Piquante -A spicy seasoned sauce often made with tomatoes and served over pasta or rice.

Sauté -To fry quickly in a small amount of oil or butter.

Shucking - To remove shells off of clams, oysters, etc.

Simmer - To cook slowly in liquid over low heat.

Tasso - Smoked pork used to season vegetables, seafood, pastas and gumbo.

Tony Chachere's -Famous Creole seasoning named after author and chef.

Zatarain's fish fry - A brand of a pre-made fish fry commonly used in the Mississippi region.

Zydeco - Blues type of Cajun dance music, popular in Louisiana. Played on an accordion, guitar and violin.

We would like to know your thoughts or comments on this book. Please send to:
The Favre Family
1191 Irvin Favre Rd.
Pass Christian, MS 39571

INDEX